NORTHWARDS BY SEA

Frontispiece: *St Clair (IV)*

Northwards by Sea

Gordon Donaldson

Paul Harris Publishing

Edinburgh

This completely revised and enlarged edition first published 1978 by
Paul Harris Publishing, 25 London Street, Edinburgh.
First printing of book under same title, 1966.

ISBN 0 904505 36 7

Donaldson, Gordon
    Northwards by Sea. — 2nd ed.
    1. Shipping — Scotland — History
    I. Title
    387'.094111   HE827

    ISBN 0-904505-36-7

Printed in Great Britain by The Shetland Times Ltd.,
Lerwick, Shetland.

PREFACE TO FIRST EDITION

Books have been written about the ships which served the Western Highlands and Islands of Scotland and other parts of the coasts of the British Isles, but none has appeared before about the services to the northern coasts of Scotland and the northern isles. Yet the ships in that area played a part in the life and economy of those remote counties which has not been surpassed anywhere, and the movements of 'the steamers' were for long a focus of interest and conversation. The last generation has seen many changes, and it is right that a pattern which is now passing away should be described before it is forgotten.

The records of the North of Scotland Shipping Company were destroyed when the head office in Aberdeen was bombed during the Second World War, and it has been necessary to reconstruct the history from various sources, especially newspapers and the archives of Aberdeen Harbour Board and Leith Dock Commission, to which access was readily granted me by the respective authorities. I owe a very great deal of the assistance of many ready helpers. Mr Edmond, the General Manager of the North of Scotland Company, and Mr Scott, the Assistant General Manager, have given me such material as they still possess, including several photographs and valuable statistics about the traffic in recent years; they have also read my typescript and have made many useful comments. I read with interest and profit Mr L. H. Liddle's two articles in *Sea Breezes* on 'Northern Saints', and indeed it was those articles, and subsequent correspondence with Mr Liddle, which finally stimulated me into taking up seriously a project I had often toyed with. Mr Graeme Somner has put at my disposal his unrivalled knowledge of shipping and has helped especially in identifying some of the ships which were chartered by the Company. Mrs A. W. Russell examined the files of *The Scotsman* over several years, and Mr Brian Smith gave me information from the local press in Shetland. Captain Thomas Gifford, formerly Commodore of the North of Scotland fleet, and Mr R. M. Leask have provided me with material about episodes in the First World War. Mr Erik Smith lent me brochures relating to the Norwegian cruises. It was through the good offices of Captain Stevenson of the *St Ola* that I obtained a picture of the first *St Rognvald,* and my old friend Mr R. L. Johnson lent me a fine painting of the *St Nicholas.* Other acknowledgments appear in the List of Illustrations and in footnotes throughout the book. Some of the information given in the following pages is the result of recollections of conversations over the years, and my debt extends to many older men whom, from time to time, I have heard 'yarning' about 'the steamers'.

G.D.

PREFACE TO SECOND EDITION

Before the first edition appeared it was already apparent that we were on the threshold of radical changes, and the decade after its publication saw something like a revolution in the pattern of sea-communications. Besides adding a chapter to bring the story up to date, I have taken the opportunity to do a good deal of re-writing throughout, partly to correct errors and to incorporate additional information about both earlier and recent history. Other researchers have meantime been busy in the field, and one important book, as well as several articles, have been published. I have resisted the temptation to expand chapter 5, on the Pentland Firth and the North Isles of Orkney, for the *Days of Orkney Steam,* by Alastair and Anne Cormack, tells the story of the inter-island steamers in Orkney in a way I could not hope to do, and their book is essential reading. Likewise, while I have enjoyed many conversations with Mr Adam Robson, who has been making an exhaustive study of the first *Earl of Zetland,* I leave it to him to put into print what is going to be as complete a biography — that is the only suitable word — as any ship of her size has ever had.

Once again I have to acknowledge my debt for much ready help. Mr Alastair McRobb (who has now put into print his work on *The Second St Ola*) was especially generous in offering corrections and supplementary information out of his great store of knowledge of the 'North' boats, and several others were stimulated by the appearance of the first edition to add useful facts to those I already had. The Aberdeen management, despite all the changes, has continued to take a close interest, and I would add the names of Mr Eric Turner, the present General Manager, and Mr James Wyllie, the Passenger Manager, to those of Mr Edmond and Mr Scott; they have found time, in the midst of their busy day-to-day work, to provide an historian with statistics and photographs and encourage him in other ways. Apart from my gratitude to them for their direct help, I should like to record my appreciation of the warm welcome

I have always received from them and from the successive officers on the ships, as I have continued, over so many years now, to enjoy travelling northwards — and also southwards — by sea.

G.D.

ACKNOWLEDGMENTS

Aberdeen Art Gallery. Plate 1.
The Stuart Bruce Collection, reproduced by permission of the Director, National Maritime Museum, Greenwich. Plates 2, 8.
Shetland Library and Museum, Lerwick. Plates 3, 10, 12, 20.
Graeme Somner. Plates 23, 24, 29.
The late Captain T. Gifford. Plate 17.
Erling J. F. Clausen, Lerwick. Plate 19.
George C. MacKay, Stromness. Plate 27.
Press and Journal, Aberdeen. Dust jacket photograph.

CONTENTS

Part I

THE SERVICES

Part II

THE SHIPS

Part III

EPILOGUE

LIST OF ILLUSTRATIONS

PLANS

PART I

THE SERVICES

Chapter One

BEFORE STEAM NAVIGATION

The glimpses we have of transport to and from Orkney and Shetland before the nineteenth century indicate a pattern radically different from anything known in recent times. Shetland's trade had in earlier centuries been conducted mainly by German merchants, especially from Bremen, who bought up the fish cured by the islanders and in return supplied them with commodities not produced in the islands. There was also a good deal of coming and going between Shetland and its nearest continental neighbour, Norway. It is true that some Scottish merchants had begun to trade with the islands as early as the sixteenth century, and even Englishmen were to be found there, but the main emphasis long continued to be on the direct links with the continent of innumerable small 'ports' in Shetland.[1] Orkney developed regular communications with the Scottish mainland at an earlier date than Shetland did and it had regular trading links with Leith by the beginning of the eighteenth century: it is significant that in 1700 three commissioners of the General Assembly bound for Shetland were able to find a trader to convey them from Leith to Kirkwall (in four days), but then they had to hire a six-oared boat, and, although it was the month of May, they were storm-stayed in Sanday for a fortnight.

When the business of disposing of Shetland fish passed from the Germans to native merchant-lairds, the pattern of trade was little altered, because the continent was the main market for the fish, and ships inevitably continued to ply to and from continental ports rather than to the Scottish mainland. Just how uncertain — as well as perilous — the journey between Edinburgh and Shetland was in the middle of the eighteenth century appears again and again in the narratives of John Mill, the minister of Dunrossness. In 1740 he left Shetland for Aberdeen in a vessel which had been bound from Norway but had been driven to Shetland by stress of weather — 'very providentially', he remarked, 'as I knew of no other occasion';

B

in 1750, on the way north, he sailed to Lerwick on a vessel
which was also accustomed to trade with Hamburg; on one
occasion he was landed at Peterhead on the way south, on
another he went to Dysart to join a vessel which he hoped would
take him north; he was often in very grave danger through
heavy seas and fogs; and one of his less eventful trips took ten
days between Leith and Bressay Sound.[2] Possibly Mill was
dogged by the adverse weather which traditionally accompanies
ministers who go to sea, and others were more fortunate. At
any rate, we learn from John Harrower's *Journal* that in
December 1773 he left Lerwick on a Monday at 5 p.m. and on
Tuesday at 6 p.m. the sloop in which he was a passenger passed
Peterhead 'in a very hard squall of wind'; next morning he was
ashore at Montrose.[3]

By the end of the eighteenth century there were some signs
of a change in the pattern of communications. While there was
still considerable trade with Holland, Hamburg and Bergen, and
some ships carried cargoes of fish direct to the Mediterranean,
continental trade was declining, and, among British ports which
had connections with Shetland, Leith had become the most
important. When the minister of Dunrossness wrote an account
of his parish in the 1790s, he remarked that trade was with
Hamburg and Leith, and the minister of Walls and Sandness
said that more imports came to his parish from Leith than from
Hamburg.

Arthur Edmondston, in his account of the *Zetland Islands*
(1809), said 'There has long been a constant trade between
Lerwick and Leith, which occupies two sloops, about seventy
tons each', and added that each of them made seven trips in
the year.[4] Samuel Hibbert, who visited Shetland in 1817 and
1818, explained that the principal trade of the islands was
carried on by smacks trading from Leith not only to Lerwick
but also to ports like Burravoe, which he describes as a principal
place of resort for them. He himself made the voyage to Lerwick
in one of the smacks, in which, so he says, the accommodation
was humble but its shortcomings compensated for by the welcome which the passengers received from the captain.[5] The
schooner *Don Cossack* is mentioned as trading between Leith
and Lerwick in 1821 and the *Fidelity* in 1825. Walter Trevelyan,
who visited Shetland in 1821, and the Rev. Daniel McAllum,
who went there in 1822, both travelled from Leith on the smack

Coldstream. Even in those days the islands had their occasional sight-seeing visitors, though the first stimulus to what is now called tourism was given only after Scott's *The Pirate* was published in 1822.

In Orkney, as in Shetland, the pattern of communications was shaped largely by the exports from the islands, but, in the case of Orkney, fish was less important as an export than corn, which went to other parts of Scotland, especially the west Highlands, to Norway, Holland, Ireland and even Spain and Portugal. From Norway the ships brought back timber, from Holland they brought a great variety of utensils and foodstuffs, from the Baltic they brought flax, from Spain and Portugal they brought salt: and from ports in southern Scotland coal was imported to Orkney. Kirkwall was also for a time a busy port because of a particular kind of through traffic, since ships from the American colonies had to call at a British port before proceeding to a foreign one, and those bound for northern Europe commonly called at Kirkwall on their way to Bremen, Hamburg, Rotterdam or Amsterdam. The traffic would in any event have come to an end when the American colonies declared their independence in 1776, but it seems to have petered out before that.[6] The majority of the vessels which were engaged in the trade between Orkney and Scotland were owned in various Firth of Forth ports, but a fair number were owned in Kirkwall, Stromness and Sanday.[7] While Kirkwall was the commercial centre of the islands, Stromness in particular long continued to have its vessels trading to ports outside Orkney. From the middle of the eighteenth century onwards into the nineteenth there was an important trade between Orkney and Liverpool, to which there are references in Orcadian sources but for which Liverpool records provide the main evidence.[8] Among vessels mentioned as trading between Orkney and Leith in the years 1818-28 are the *Friends, Robina, Sir Joseph Banks, Nancy, Dispatch, Eliza, Margaret* and *George Canning;* the *Dispatch* and the *Margaret* belonged to Stromness, the others evidently to Kirkwall.

The dangers of the sea passage are illustrated time and again. In 1794, Robert Stevenson, the lighthouse engineer, sailed from Orkney in the sloop *Elizabeth,* of Stromness; he left her at Kinnaird Head, after which she was driven back to Orkney and lost. One of the disasters which seems to have been best remembered was the wreck of the *Doris,* off Aberdeen, with loss of life, in 1813. The recurrent anxiety about vessels which were overdue comes out in the correspondence of the Wesleyan missionaries who were active in Shetland in the 1820s.[9] A letter dated 10 December 1822, referring to the *Coldstream,* states that 'there is great reason to conclude that she was lost on her passage up, and that all on board, consisting of eight passengers and crew, found in the deep one common grave'.[10] Another, dated 21 March 1825, reads: 'it appears that all our preceding letters, for some months, have been lost; a little vessel that had sailed from Leith with the mail to Lerwick, about two months ago, having never been heard of since. Mr Hindson, who was sent to supply the place of him "who had departed from the work" was to have sailed in that vessel, but was providentially prevented. He waited for another vessel, and arrived safely, in less than three days' sail'.[11] Three days from Lerwick to Leith was not a record, as a diary of a voyage on the *Coldstream* in 1822 shows. Going north, she left Leith on Monday, 24 June at 5 p.m. and anchored in Bressay Sound at 1.30 p.m. on Thursday, after being unable to land a passenger at Fair Isle at 3 a.m. because of the rough sea and succeeding in landing a passenger at Quendale at 9 a.m. On the way south she did even better: left Lerwick on 10 July at 1 p.m. and arrived at Leith on 12 July at 10 p.m. — 57 hours.

It happens that we have particularly full information for 1828-9, just a few years before the appearance of steam navigation to the islands, and a detailed account can be given of the situation as it was then. The principal traffic was now by smacks trading to Leith. Between Kirkwall and Leith, some of those smacks achieved a fairly regular service roughly once each month, at least in summer. Thus, the *Sir Joseph Banks,* of 79 tons, registered at Kirkwall, arrived at Leith on 26 May, 25 June, 21 July, 3 September, 2 October, 1 November, 22 December, 10 February and 25 March, and the *George Canning,* of 91 tons, also registered at Kirkwall, arrived at Leith on 4 June, 5 July, 24 July, 9 August, 15 September, 17 October, 29 November and 3 January. In addition, the *Medora* (33 tons) made three trips between May and January and the following made one each; *Nancy* (86 tons), *Regent* (142), *Flora* (63), *Despatch* (37), *Brisk* (76), *Fisher* (58), *Elizabeth and Samuel* (55), *George* (33), *Margaret* (61) and *William Bowers* (38). In all, this worked out at an average of about three arrivals in Leith from Kirkwall each month. There was also a regular trader from Stromness, another *Margaret* (64 tons), which arrived at Leith in May, June, October, November and January; and the *James* arrived from Stromness on 17 October. It must, of course, be kept in mind that such vessels were trading to many other ports besides Leith, and some of them turn up occasionally in Liverpool, for example: the *Dispatch* in 1809, *Nancy* in 1814 and *Robina* (mentioned later) in 1814.

Among the smacks from Shetland to Leith the most regular was the schooner *Norna* (87 tons), belonging to the Leith and Shetland Shipping Company, which seems to have aimed at a six-weeks schedule and which arrived at Leith on 28 June, 14 August, 4 October, 29 November, 31 January and 7 March. The *Fidelity* (125 tons) arrived on 5 July, 3 September, 5 January and 13 March, the *Helen* (53 tons) on 21 July, 15 September, 3 November and 25 December, and the *Dolphin* (56 tons) on 14 July and 27 August. In addition, the following made occasional trips: *Mary L. Mason* (42 tons), *Perseverance* (25), *Rose* (28), *Mary Ann* (29), *Albion* (42), *Argyll* (42), *Morpark* (35), *Margaret* (76) and *Jessy* (20). In all, the average number of arrivals in a month was not more than two, except in September, when there were seven, and in October, when there were six, no doubt because of heavy exports of fish.

While Leith was clearly the main destination of the Orkney and Shetland smacks, some of them occasionally made a trip to Aberdeen. Thus, in November 1827, the *Dolphin* and the *George Canning,* both owned at Lerwick, and the *Janet,* owned at Aberdeen, each left Aberdeen for Lerwick, and the *Pomona Packet,* of Stromness, left Aberdeen for Stromness on 20 December. In 1828 there were the following sailings from Aberdeen to Lerwick with general cargo: the *Marquis of Huntly* of Aberdeen in April, the *Adventure* of Aberdeen in May, the *Catherine* of Aberdeen in June and the *Barbara* of Lerwick in September; in addition, the *Cecilia* of Lerwick sailed for her home port with meal in April, and in September two ships left Aberdeen for Lerwick with herring barrels. The *Robina* of Kirkwall sailed for her home port in December 1828, and in June 1829 there were three arrivals at Aberdeen from Kirkwall: the *Pomona Packet,* the *Elizabeth and Samuel* and the *Margaret,* all owned in Orkney.

The Orkney mail service was quite apart from, and independent of, the main freight service by the smacks. The system of roads throughout the north and west of Scotland, constructed by the Commissioners for Highland Roads and Bridges, at last reached Thurso, and a mail coach to that town started in 1819. This greatly facilitated communication with Orkney by way of the Pentland Firth, though then and for some years to come there was still no road from either Wick or Thurso to Huna (about three miles west of Duncansby Head), the point from which the Orkney mail boat left. The arrangements for the actual crossing, too, were still very primitive. One who made it in 1790 records: 'Sailed from Houna about seven in the morning in a small boat with four men, who rowed almost the whole time with a small sail, and I steered; passed between Stroma and Pentland Skerries, and between Swona and South Ronaldsha, and about ten landed at Burwick in the last-mentioned island'.[12] Even in 1828 there was no harbour at Huna and 'the only means of conveying the mail' was by 'a row-boat of small dimensions'. And as the boat landed on the shores of South Ronaldsay, two further ferries, on each side of Burray, had still to be crossed before the Orkney mainland was reached.

If Orkney had a regular mail service, however inefficient, Shetland had none at all. Several efforts had been made to obtain such a service,[13] and undertakings were sometimes given to deliver mail in Shetland ten or twelve times a year. Edmondston referred in 1809 to 'a packet which carries the mail' between Aberdeen and Lerwick, which was supposed to leave Aberdeen on the first Sunday of every month except December and January, but the government grant was too small to permit of such regularity in practice. It was stated in 1828 that 'the Shetlanders depend altogether upon chance-ships or trading vessels for their letters', and Robert Stevenson, the Inspector of Northern Lights, remarked that even in the best season of the year he had brought news to Lerwick which had already been current for six weeks in the south of Scotland. Besides, although Orkney and Shetland at that time formed parts of a single county, transport between them was 'perhaps as little as if the expanse of the Atlantic separated them'. Anyone going from one to the other had either to charter a vessel or else travel to Leith by one smack and then proceed north again by another.

In a proposal which Stevenson made for a Shetland mail service by way of Orkney he anticipated the kind of island-hopping service which has recently been introduced in the western isles by the car-ferries. His suggestion was that from a harbour to be constructed on the Caithness coast a packet should operate to the mainland of Orkney; from Kirkwall there should be an improved packet to Sanday; and from Otterswick in Sanday there should be a service to Scalloway. He considered that Orkney could thus have a post at least thrice a week and Shetland could have one once a week.[13] Stevenson's proposal might charitably be characterised as over-ingenious, but it is the kind of plan which might be drawn up by some official who has looked at a map but has paid no attention to local wishes or conditions or to the manner in which commercial ties have evolved and become established. At any rate, nothing came of such a hare-brained project, and in 1833 the Shetland mails 'were despatched and received by chance coasting vessels at the rate of a penny a letter; six and eight weeks often elapsed between opportunities, and when a mail was to be made up, sometimes at a moment's notice, the bellman was sent hastily through the streets of Lerwick'. And it was still true, just before the steamers arrived to transform the situation, that between Shetland and Orkney there was 'no trade communication whatever'.[14]

Although steam was to appear soon after 1828, the new method of propulsion was far from driving the smacks at once out of business. On the contrary, sailing vessels played an important part in communications with the islands for nearly another half century; in fact, for many years there was no appreciable reduction in the number of trips by sailing vessels, and it is clear that the steamers, whatever their contribution to the mail service, made no immediate impact on the general pattern of communications. The sailing vessels which were operated by the steamer company and supplemented its service will be mentioned in the following chapter, but something may be said here about the other vessels, mostly owned in the islands, which continued to ply.

In 1845-6 some of the sailing vessels which had traded in 1827-8 were still running, and some additional ones were also operating. Thus the *Sir Joseph Banks* was still making a monthly run, at least in summer, between Kirkwall and Leith. Besides, the *Mary Balfour* (50 tons) made the trip every three weeks; the

Thomas and Mary (19), the *Mary Trail* (55) and the *Paragon*
(83) made the trip occasionally. There were two arrivals from
Kirkwall in May, three in June, three in July and two in August.
Between Stromness and Leith the *Magnet* (50 tons) plied
monthly in summer and occasionally at other seasons, and an
early holder of a familiar name, the *Earl of Zetland* (79 tons)
also sailed occasionally. Between Lerwick and Leith the most
important trader was now the schooner *Magnus Troil,* which,
being of 110 tons, was larger than most earlier smacks. She
belonged to the Zetland New Shipping Company and had been
in service in 1832 and in 1837, when Arthur Robertson was her
master. In 1845 she arrived in Leith on 29 May, 14 July and
14 August. The *Three Sisters* (66 tons) arrived from Lerwick on
23 June and 5 August. The *Margaret* and the *Dolphin* were still
trading occasionally, as they had done in 1827-8, and the *Norna,*
which had been lost on the Blue Mull of Unst in 1839, had
been replaced by a smaller vessel of the same name. There were
two arrivals in all from Lerwick in each of the four months
from May to August. Winter services to both Orkney and
Shetland were much less regular, for in January 1846 there were
hardly any arrivals at Leith from the islands except the *Queen of*
the Isles (87 tons) from Lerwick, but in February there were
four arrivals from Lerwick.

It was in 1846 that one of the best-remembered and most
successful of the sailing ships which plied between Leith and
Lerwick made her appearance. She was the *Matchless,* built for
the Zetland New Shipping Company. The builders, Alexander
Hall and Company, of Aberdeen, had recently pioneered the
clipper type of ship, beginning with the *Scottish Maid,* built in
1839 to compete with the steamships between Scottish ports
and London, and the *Matchless* was built on lines identical with
that vessel.[15] She was a two-masted schooner, 89 feet long, 18
feet broad and 11.4 feet deep — all internal measurements —
and of 107 tons. The accommodation included a ladies' cabin,
with four berths, and a roomy fore-cabin, in which the fare from
Lerwick to Leith was 5s. The vessel proved so speedy and
reliable that she was able to continue to trade between Lerwick
and Leith, despite the competition of steam, until so late as
1882. She could do the run in 24 hours under good conditions
and is said to have logged as much as 13½ knots, but did not
make such speeds without sometimes shipping a lot of water.

1. *Sovereign*

2. *Queen (II)*

3. *St Magnus (I)* and *Earl of Zetland (I)*

St. Clair (1)

A member of the crew, asked if she was a wet ship, replied, 'Weet? Man, weet is no da wird for yün. She gaed doon aff Buchan Ness an' cam' up aff Sumburgh Heid'. She seems to have made a monthly trip with unfailing regularity, for in 1863 she was turning up in Leith on about the same date each month: 7 July, 10 August, 10 September, 9 October and 9 November. Her captain then was John William Petrie, and other skippers were William Scott and Robert Nisbet. Only in 1883 (by which date Shetland had three steamers weekly in summer and two in winter) was the *Matchless* disposed of, to South African owners.

Other sailing vessels trading between Leith and Shetland in 1863 were the *Imogen* (57 tons), *Petrel* (51), *Sage* (39) and the *Queen of the Isles* already mentioned. The *Reaper* was trading to Stromness, the *Pandora* and the *Paragon* to Kirkwall. The two last-named were advertised about that time as 'the only direct conveyance between' Leith and Kirkwall (for the steamers, of course, called at Aberdeen); sailings were on Thursday from Leith and Friday from Kirkwall, and the fares were — cabin, 10s. 6d. (with provisions 15s.), steerage 6s., as compared with the steamer fares of 18s. and 8s.

The *Queen of the Isles* had been built at Leith a year before the *Matchless* appeared in 1846, and she continued after the *Matchless* was withdrawn. In 1875 an interest in this vessel was acquired by Captain Nisbet, who had been in command of the *Matchless* for ten years and had before that, for a few months in 1864, skippered the *Imogen,* trading to the North Isles of Shetland. The *Queen of the Isles* had for some time been running to the west side of Shetland, which was still without a steamer service, and Nisbet commanded her on this trade for five years, until, at the request of the North of Scotland Company, he accepted the command of their steamer, *Queen.* Possibly there is some connection between the appointment of this experienced captain and the fact that in 1881 the *Queen* became the first steamer to serve the west-side ports. At any rate, the *Queen of the Isles,* while no longer required on the west side after 1881, continued to trade between Leith and Lerwick or Kirkwall until she was broken up in March 1899.

The *Queen of the Isles* was not the only sailing vessel which outlived the *Matchless* and survived after a fairly full schedule of steamer services was established. In 1881 the schooner *Vic-*

toria was trading between various places in Shetland and ports as far away as Liverpool and Seaham. The *Luna* and the *Pomona* traded regularly between Leith and Kirkwall in 1884-6 and in September 1885 the smack *Noran* was advertised to sail from Leith to Scalloway and the west side of Shetland. The *Pomona*, at least, was running up to 1900. The *Mersey*, a former Liverpool pilot cutter, built in 1847, and used by Peter Tait of Scalloway in the Faroe fishing from 1875 to 1894, was sold to William Smith in the latter year and operated between Shetland and the south until shortly before she was broken up in 1909. But it was inevitable that as the steamship service became more frequent and reliable the sailing ships would gradually disappear from the northern islands.

REFERENCES

1 See G. Donaldson, *Shetland Life under Earl Patrick*, 59-72.
2 *Diary of Rev. John Mill* (Scottish History Society), 2, 7, 29-30.
3 *Journal of John Harrower*, ed. Edward M. Riley (Colonial Williamsburg, 1965).
4 Edmondston, ii, 18, 21.
5 Hibbert, *Description of the Shetland Islands* (1931), 3-4, 193.
6 Rosalind Mitchison, 'Two northern ports', in *Scottish Studies*, vii, 75-82.
7 Hugh Marwick, *Merchant lairds of long ago* (1939).
8 I am indebted for this information to Mr Ronald Mooney.
9 Vol. xiii of the *Miscellaneous Works* of Adam Clarke, published in 1837, contains a 'Brief History of the Zetland Isles', 'Missionary Correspondence' and Clarke's own 'Journal', which give a remarkable picture of Shetland's communications. As a rule the travellers depended on the normal traders, but in 1828 it appears that a group of Wesleyans made special arrangements to sail on the *Henry* from Whitby to Lerwick, round the islands and then back to Sunderland. I am indebted to Mr Peter Jamieson, of Lerwick, for drawing my attention to this important source.
10 Clarke's *Works*, xiii, 142.
11 *Ibid.*, 231.
12 *Innes Review*, vi (1955), 140-1.
13 *Fourteenth Report of Commission on Highland Roads and Bridges* (1828), especially page 45. A somewhat similar proposal appeared in the Orkney press in the early 1860s.
14 R. L. Stevenson, *Records of a Family of Engineers* (Tusitala Edition), 196.
15 The *Matchless* is illustrated in an article in *Sea Breezes*, March 1933, the *Scottish Maid* in Victoria Clark, *History of the Port of Aberdeen*.

Chapter Two

THE EARLY DAYS OF STEAM

When we begin to study the origins of steam navigation in the
north of Scotland and the northern isles, the emphasis shifts
from the islands themselves, and from Leith, because Aberdeen
was the headquarters of the company which developed steam
navigation up the Scottish east coast. The company had existed
since 1790, at first as the Leith and Clyde Shipping Company,
and, after its amalgamation in 1810 with the Aberdeen, Dundee
and Leith Shipping Company, as the Aberdeen, Leith, Clyde and
Tay Shipping Company, or, more shortly, the Aberdeen, Leith
and Clyde. The company's advertisements made use also of a
number of variations which indicated either specific aspects of
the trade or the existence of subsidiary enterprises, such as
'Inverness and Leith Steam Packet Company' and other names
mentioning Caithness and the Moray Firth, and it is difficult
to disentangle these from the similar names used by unrelated
companies. The Aberdeen, Leith and Clyde became the North
of Scotland and Orkney and Shetland Steam Navigation Company in June 1873 and, though it became a public company
in 1919, retained that title until in 1953 its name was changed
to the North of Scotland, Orkney and Shetland Shipping Company Ltd.; the old term 'Shipping Company', which had been
used in the era before steam navigation, was then revived
because motor vessels by that time predominated in the company's fleet.

While the company had its headquarters in Aberdeen, it
was from the beginning concerned with Leith as well, and
throughout nearly all its long history Leith or an adjacent port
was the southern terminal point of most of the main-line services.
It appears, however, that in the 1820s and 1830s what was
called Leith included piers at Newhaven and that it was from
Newhaven that the steamships mostly operated, possibly because
it offered wharfage less dependent on the state of the tides than
the docks at Leith. More oddly still, although the Aberdeen
Harbour Board Records always show Leith as the terminal point

except from the summer of 1866 until October 1879, when Granton is named instead, it appears from other evidence that Granton in fact became the terminal from 1840 to 1880, when Leith finally took its place. Until after the Second World War, the vessels worked from the Albert Dock and Albert Wharf, but then the Company took over the Victoria Wharf, vacated by the London and Edinburgh Shipping Company. It was, however, the all but invariable practice for the steamers to call at Aberdeen on their passages to and from the islands, partly because Aberdeen was the port for handling the mails.[1]

In its early days, the Company's trade was continental as well as coastal, and was carried on by smacks like the *Glasgow Packet* (82 tons), built by Alexander Hall and Company in 1811, and the *Edinburgh Packet,* built by them in 1812. In 1820 the Company had eight such smacks, and their *Marquis of Huntly* was normally on a Leith-Aberdeen service from at least 1822 to 1828. The Company's first interest in steam arose in connection with the passage between Aberdeen and Leith, when paddle steamers started to augment the service offered by the Company's smacks. The Leith and Aberdeen Steam Yacht Company introduced the *Tourist,* of 257 tons, in May 1821, but she was soon transferred to the Leith-London route and replaced by the *Brilliant.* In July of the same year there appeared the *Velocity,* owned by the Aberdeen, Leith and Clyde under the name Aberdeen and Leith Steam Yacht Company. The two rival firms agreed to run their vessels on alternate days, and for a few months they each made the return trip thrice weekly, giving almost a daily service. As the years passed there were variations, but thrice weekly seems to have been found to be more than the traffic would stand, and the general pattern after 1822 was of two sailings weekly by each ship. An advertisement of 1824 indicates the time-table. The 'steam yacht *Velocity,* Andrew Crane commander', sailed from Newhaven for Aberdeen on Thursdays and Saturdays at 6 a.m. and from Aberdeen for Newhaven on Tuesdays and Fridays at the same hour. On the way, the vessel called off Elie and Anstruther, Crail, Arbroath, Montrose, Johnshaven and Stonehaven to embark and disembark passengers, and with these interruptions the passage could take about twelve hours, but in April 1823 the *Velocity* is recorded as making it in ten hours on her first trip of the season, while the *Brilliant* made it in 10¾ hours, against the wind and including the time spent in making six calls. The cabin fare (single) was 21s., the steerage 12s. As the term 'steam yacht' suggests, the service was essentially for passengers (while the smacks would continue to carry cargo), and for several years the steamers were withdrawn from the Leith-Aberdeen service in winter; only in 1838 did they begin to ply regularly throughout the year.

In 1826 the Leith, Aberdeen and Clyde bought the *Brilliant* and they soon began to find other uses for both her and the *Velocity* in addition to the passage between Aberdeen and Leith. For a few years a pattern of expansion was steadily pursued, as the steamers pushed ever farther north, first in summer, then in winter, at first fortnightly, later weekly. From the outset the *Brilliant* had made occasional trips to Inverness and Cromarty and in 1828 the *Velocity* made a run to Wick. In the summer of 1829 the *Brilliant* was on a regular weekly run from Leith to Aberdeen and Inverness, and she continued that each year until 1838. In the summer of that year, the *Brilliant* and the *Velocity* were both making weekly runs from Leith to Aberdeen and Inverness, and the Company evidently had competition, for a vessel appropriately called the *Satellite* was following exactly the same schedule as the *Velocity*. After 1838 the Inverness service was as a rule only once weekly, but the Company evidently regarded it as their premier route, for the new *Duke of Richmond* succeeded the *Brilliant* in the autumn of 1838 and maintained this run until 1852, when the *Queen* (I), a newer vessel, took her place. This service disappeared, however, after the summer of 1859, except for a resumption by the *Queen* (II) from April 1874 until the end of that year. In winter, sailings to and from Inverness seem to have been irregular, mainly by sailing vessels, until the end of 1848. From the winter of 1849-50 until the winter of 1857-8, however, there was a weekly service, just as in summer, maintained by the same steamships.

From 1829 until 1832, each summer, the *Velocity* was employed only on a twice-weekly run to and from Leith, with an occasional trip to Wick (as in 1828). In the summer of 1833, however, the voyage to Wick became a regular feature every fortnight, and in the same year the islands were reached by steam, for the *Velocity* proceeded to Kirkwall as well as Wick on her runs north, from June to August. A similar schedule, leaving Aberdeen on alternative Fridays for Wick and Kirkwall, continued in 1834 from the month of June to the beginning of September, and in 1835 from 22 May until 11 September.

In the summer of 1836 there was a significant change, with the advent of the *Sovereign,* which made her first appearance at the end of June. Each week from 11 July to 5 September she left Newhaven and Aberdeen for the north, not on Friday, as before, but on Monday. She went as far as Wick and Kirkwall every week, and ventured to Lerwick fortnightly. It is said that she called briefly at Lerwick on alternate Wednesday afternoons, and this fits in with her times of departure from Aberdeen. Her last trip to Lerwick for the season was on 29 August. In 1837 she appears to have had the same schedule, for she was leaving Aberdeen for Wick each Monday from the beginning of July until the beginning of October and leaving Aberdeen for Leith each Friday. The *Brilliant* meantime was leaving Aberdeen for Inverness on Tuesdays and for Leith on Saturdays, and the *Velocity* was running twice weekly between Aberdeen and Leith.

The year 1838 was one of the more significant in the Company's history. It was at this point that a government contract was obtained for the conveyance of mails to and from Shetland once a week in summer (April-October) by steamship. The summer run to Lerwick therefore now became a weekly one, and its schedule was one which was long to remain familiar. The *Sovereign* was now leaving Leith every Friday for Aberdeen, Wick, Kirkwall and Lerwick, and leaving Lerwick on Monday, Kirkwall and Wick on Tuesday. In this time-table we have essentially that of 'the week-end boat', which remained the primary service to Orkney and Shetland for a hundred and one years, until 1939 — though Wick ceased to be a normal port of call on this run after the summer of 1891. Only after the Second World War was this service demoted to a secondary place and terminated at Kirkwall for eight months of the year.

An advertisement in July 1838 gives the full programme of the Company's steamers: sailings from Leith or Newhaven to Aberdeen on Tuesday, Thursday, Friday and Saturday at 6 a.m. and from Aberdeen for Newhaven or Leith on Monday, Wednesday, Friday and Saturday at 6 a.m. The *Brilliant,* which left for the north on Tuesday, was billed for Inverness as well as Aberdeen, and the *Sovereign,* which sailed on Friday, for Shetland.

To make a trip by steamer to the most northerly town in the British Isles was a novel attraction to enterprising travellers, and the *Sovereign,* though a paddle steamer of only 378 gross tons, was highly thought of at the time by those who travelled in her. Catherine Sinclair, who went north in 1839 from Wick to Lerwick, called her 'a fine, large, well-grown steamboat'.[2] Miss Sinclair, after a stay in Lerwick from Saturday night to Monday evening, was less favourably impressed on the return voyage to Wick, when the only passenger able to sit down to dinner with Captain Phillips was Christian Ployen, the governor of Faroe, who happened to be travelling from Lerwick (which he tells us he left about 6 p.m. on Monday, 17 June) to Aberdeen (where he arrived about 6 a.m. on Wednesday).[3]

It seemed in 1838 that a weekly run by a steamer to Lerwick might continue throughout the winter, for after trips by the *Sovereign,* leaving Aberdeen on Saturdays 10 and 17 November, the *Duke of Richmond* took over and made weekly runs until the end of the year. This, however, was not maintained, and, although the steamer service continued each summer, Shetland continued to be served in succeeding winters, for another twenty years, by sailing vessels, which carried the mails on an approximately fortnightly schedule. The mail contract, which provided for a Shetland mail weekly in summer, laid down that in winter the mail should be conveyed by sailing vessels only as often as the weather should permit. Thus in the winter of 1838-9 the *Aberdeen Packet* left Aberdeen for Lerwick on 4, 16 and 29 January, 2 and 21 February and 12, 20 and 29 March, and at the end of 1843 she left Aberdeen for Lerwick on 30 November, 13 and 24 December. In the winters from 1848-9 to 1851-2 the *William Hogarth* maintained a service roughly twice a month. From the winter of 1852-3 this duty fell to the top-sail schooner *Fairy,*[4] which carried it on until the winter of 1859-60. This sailing vessel's last run to Lerwick from Aberdeen was on 2 March 1860.

The fact is that although steamships had been operated by the Company since the 1820s, sail long continued to play an important part in its general programme. Thus, in the summer of 1843, while the steamers *Sovereign, Duke of Richmond* and *Bonnie Dundee* were carrying out services between Leith and Inverness, Leith and Lerwick and Leith and Aberdeen respectively (the last twice weekly), the Company was still employing

a number of smaller sailing vessels: the *Fairy* (150 tons) between
Leith and Aberdeen weekly, the *Liverpool Packet* (81 tons) and
the *Glasgow Packet* (73) between Aberdeen and Glasgow fortnightly, the *Dahlia* (73) and the *Courier* (66) between Aberdeen
and Glasgow every three weeks, and the *Belmont* (75) between
Aberdeen and Grangemouth. In 1850, when the Company had
seven steamers (for the *Queen* (I), the *Victoria*, the *Newhaven*
and the *Hamburg* had been added to the fleet), it was still
operating the *Fairy*, the *Dee*, the *Don*, the *Liverpool Packet*,
the *Dahlia* and the *William Hogarth*.

Besides, the whole problem of regular all-year services by
steamers was a difficult one, and one which was only slowly
solved. Down to 1848 the only regular steam service in winter
was still that between Leith and Aberdeen. As already
mentioned, the regular winter steamer service to Inverness was
not established until 1848-9. In the next winter but one,
1850-1, a weekly steamer service from Leith and Aberdeen to
Wick and Kirkwall was operating, leaving Aberdeen on Friday
and returning on Wednesday; this was the same schedule as that
of the service which went on to Shetland in the summer. A
second winter run to Wick began in 1857-8. A fortnightly
steamer to Lerwick in winter started in 1858-9, though for two
seasons it did not supersede the *Fairy*. The winter steamer at
first left Aberdeen on Saturday or Sunday and returned to
Aberdeen on Friday, but from the end of 1860 the winter service
became a weekly one, on a schedule more or less as in summer.
Even so, however, it appears that departures and arrivals were
in practice far from regular, and it may well be that steamships
were still proving unsatisfactory in those northern seas in winter.
The steamer which, it had been hoped, would be successful in
the winter service to the islands was the *Prince Consort*. With
the exception of the *Hamburg*, which the Company had owned
from 1849 to 1852, she was their first iron ship; she was, with
the same exception, their largest ship to date; and her horse-
power was 300. She had started running in March 1858, but the
Sovereign shared her work with her. However, the *Prince Consort*
was still a paddler, and it is obvious to reason that no paddle
steamer could operate successfully and regularly in winter. It
was only with the acquisition of the screw steamer *Queen* (II),
which arrived at Lerwick on her first trip on 9 November 1861,
that a satisfactory winter service became practicable. It seems a

little odd that after 1861 the Company was still to acquire two more paddlers — the *Vanguard* in 1863, the first *St Magnus* in 1867 — but paddlers had advantages of speed and shallow draught; it is noticeable, however, that the *Vanguard* was kept for only two years and that the *St Magnus* was little used in winter. Another difficulty in the way of regular winter services was probably the lack of lighthouses: it is, at any rate, notable that the first regular winter steamer service to Lerwick started after the appearance of the light on Bressay in 1858.

In summer, the service to Lerwick, *via* Wick and Kirkwall, once a week, was the only service north of Inverness until 1850, though its importance is suggested by the fact that the new and larger *Queen* (I) was allotted to it in 1845. In 1850 an additional summer service was provided for Wick each week, leaving Leith on Mondays, and in 1852 this was extended to Scrabster (Thurso). Like the 'weekend-boat' to Orkney and Shetland, this service too had a lifetime of about a century, for during most of that period a vessel left Leith each week for Aberdeen, Wick and Thurso, and a Monday departure was normal. In 1857-8, as already mentioned, the extra run to Wick continued throughout the winter, giving Wick for a time two steamers a week in winter.

In the early 1860s the Company's activities were very restricted. The Inverness service had come to an end in 1859 and there was as yet no expansion to speak of further north. In summer and winter alike there were only two steamer services weekly — one from Leith on Monday or Tuesday morning to Aberdeen, Wick and Thurso, the other from Leith on Friday morning to Aberdeen, Wick, Kirkwall and Lerwick. Indeed, the Company had no more than three steamers in active use at this point — the *Bonnie Dundee* had been sold in 1853 and was not replaced; the *Queen* (I) had been lost in 1857 and was replaced by the *Prince Consort;* the *Duke of Richmond* was lost in 1859 and her place was taken by the *Hamburg* until the advent of the *Queen* (II) in 1861; and the *Sovereign* was not disposed of until 1865 but was in effect superseded by the *Vanguard* in 1863.

Very soon after 1860, however, the Company entered on a phase of remarkable development. Possibly it should really be dated from the appearance of the first screw steamer, the *Queen* of 1861, but it is a curious coincidence that it was associated with the initiation of the practice of giving the ships the names

C

of saints, beginning with the *St Magnus* in 1867, the *St Clair* in 1868 and the *St Nicholas* in 1871. While not all of the ships so called have been lucky individually, there is no doubt that collectively they have amply justified the happy choice first made in 1867. The three earliest 'saints', added to the *Queen* of 1861, made an outstandingly up-to-date fleet.

The first innovation of the period of expansion was an additional sailing to the islands in summer. From 1866, besides the 'weekend-boat', arriving in Aberdeen from Lerwick on Wednesday and from Granton on Friday, there was another vessel, arriving from Lerwick on Friday or Saturday and from Granton on Tuesday. This new sailing was what can be called the 'secondary indirect boat', which, with schedules which altered slightly from time to time, was a feature of the summer programmes in most seasons until 1939. In 1946 a time-table based on a departure from Leith on Monday and a return on Saturday became that of the principal indirect boat all the year round.

The next step in expansion was the extension of Stornoway, at least as an occasional feature, of the programme of the Wick and Thurso sailing. This is recorded for the first time in the summer of 1861, and it was to remain part of the programme, with varying frequency and regularity, for upwards of forty years. It is not clear how far it was ever the intention to try to establish a connection between the Western Isles and Aberdeen which could compete seriously with their well-established service to Glasgow, but we do find the *Queen* making an isolated trip (with cattle) to Lochboisdale in July 1879 and a special trip to Stornoway in November of that year. And it must have been realised that the distance from Stornoway to Aberdeen is actually rather less than that from Stornoway to Glasgow. Another sign of activity was the revival, in 1874, of a service to Inverness, after a lapse of fifteen years, but this was not maintained, and only an occasional isolated run to Inverness is to be found in later years, as by the *St Clair* in November 1884. There is no doubt that the Company was at this stage looking around for additional business, but it was not to find it on the mainland or in the western isles.

It was agreed in March 1881 that Shetland should have three mails a week in summer and two in winter. A third weekly run to Shetland in summer therefore began in 1881 — from Leith on Monday morning to Aberdeen, Stromness and

Scalloway — and this soon became the full 'west-side service', proceeding beyond Scalloway to other ports on the west side of Shetland, a service which continued with minor variations until 1939. As mentioned in the previous chapter, the Company probably benefited from the experience of Captain Nisbet, who had previously skippered the *Queen of the Isles* in those waters, and experience was certainly necessary in the tortuous channels of the west side of Shetland. It is related that Captain Nisbet had various private arrangements to compensate for the lack of official lights: a lamp in a crofter's cottage enabled him to make his way through Vaila Sound into Walls, and a lamp in the staircase window of Melby House helped him through Papa Sound — a service which he acknowledged with a blast on the whistle as he passed.

The minor west-side ports — apart, that is, from Scalloway — were Spiggie, Walls, Brae, Voe, Aith and Hillswick; and, although they do not appear to be mentioned in the schedules, Reawick and Roeness Voe certainly received calls from time to time — the latter being especially important when many herring were being cured at the stations on its shores. The pattern of calls varied much over the years, and at times each of the minor ports had only a fortnightly, or even a monthly, call. Scalloway and Walls had piers which could accommodate the steamers, but at the other ports passengers and goods had to be boated to and from the shore. After the First World War the only ports between Scalloway and Hillswick were Walls, Brae, Voe and Aith, and they were abandoned stage by stage in the 1920s and 1930s until they had all disappeared by 1937. During a good part of her career, the west-side boat called fortnightly at St Margaret's Hope.

The provision of an additional winter service seems to have caused some difficulty. In the winter of 1881-2 there were certainly two vessels running to Shetland, but even the timetable showed much variation and the actual sailings seem to have been somewhat erratic. In that winter and the two or three which followed, the second winter sailing was sometimes to Lerwick (*via* Stromness), sometimes to Scalloway, and only after some time did the west-side service become an invariable winter feature. The little *Queen,* of 448 tons, must often have found the stretch of ocean between Stromness and Scalloway more than she could face, and it is not surprising that on Monday, 19

December 1881, *The Scotsman* carried an announcement that 'The steamship *Queen* has been detained in Shetland by stormy weather and will not sail from Leith tonight'. However, from 1881-2 Shetland had its two winter services.

The North of Scotland Company, while it had no major competitor in the development of the steamer service to the islands, was not quite alone. From about 1870 the Iceland and Faroe mail steamer from Copenhagen called at Lerwick in April, May, June and September — a pattern almost repeated for a few years after the Second World War, when the Faroe mail vessel, the *Tjaldur,* called similarly at Lerwick. From time to time, too, the steamer bound from Leith to Iceland would call at Lerwick and then proceed north through Yellsound. More regular, however, and more used by British passengers, were the sailings of Langlands' steamers, which, on their service between Liverpool and Leith, instituted in 1874, called once a week at Stromness until 1914. As they had several calls *en route* in both directions — Oban, Stornoway, Aberdeen and Dundee — they did not provide a speedy passage from the mainland to Orkney, but they were popular with holiday-makers who wanted a leisurely cruise.

Intermittent efforts were made by Orcadian interests, with some success, to compete in the Kirkwall-Leith traffic,[5] and on the Leith-Shetland run the most determined effort made to offer a direct challenge to the North of Scotland Company was made by the Shetland Islands Steam Trading Company Ltd., which was formed as a result of a public meeting called at Lerwick on 12 November 1902.[6] It was pointed out that as a result of an experiment by Orcadians in putting on 'a boat of their own' the Company had reduced their freight rates to Orkney, and it was hoped that the same would be achieved in Shetland. The threat of independent action in Shetland produced an immediate response in an offer by the Company to reduce freights by about 15%, but this was not considered satisfactory, and the Lerwick committee went ahead to collect subscriptions from prospective shareholders. The sums promised came from all parts of the islands and from people in the south, and ranged from £500 down to £1. In January 1903 it was resolved to call up 25% of the offered capital in order to charter a ship and then to call up the remainder in order to purchase her should she prove satisfactory. The Company chartered the *Mona* and the *Trojan* in 1903; in 1904 they acquired the steamer *Norseman* (430 tons), which ran from Leith on Mondays to Aberdeen, Wick, Lerwick and the North Isles with goods and passengers, and they also operated for a time the *Helen* and the *Earlford*. Already before the end of 1904 the Company's financial position was so weak that the Finance Committee welcomed the prospect of saving 13s. 8d. a week in harbour dues and reduced the salaries of the office staff. It was much to their disadvantage that the *Norseman,* almost as soon as she was acquired, had to have costly repairs. Profits were made in the fishing season, but not outside it. By June 1907 there was a debit balance of over £6000. The Company seems to have ceased operations later in that year.[7] In the same period as the *Norseman,* there was another rival to the 'North' Company: in 1905 the cargo steamer *Matje* (280 tons), under the Leith and East Coast Steam Shipping Company, was trading from Leith to Aberdeen, Wick, Scrabster and Macduff.

It is clear that there had been a period when expansion of the steamship services had been very rapid — startlingly rapid when one recalls that until 1858 Shetland did not have a steamer in winter at all, and only one in summer, whereas by 1883 Shetland had three steamers in summer and two in winter. Moreover, as will appear in the next chapter, expansion was to continue fairly steadily for another thirty years. The economic background is to be found in the very profound changes which were gradually coming over the nature of life in the islands. In the early nineteenth century the islands had been very largely self-supporting, in food, clothing and fuel, though imports of corn to Shetland and of luxury articles to both groups of islands were always necessary. By the end of the nineteenth century, almost all clothing, a very wide range of foodstuffs and considerable quantities of coal, besides utensils, timber and other commodities, were being imported, and life in the islands was very dependent on such imports. There was relatively little to export in return, and the operation of transport to the islands has always laboured under the disadvantage that the traffic is largely one-way and the freight charges must therefore of necessity pay for a double voyage. Hosiery from Shetland, eggs from Orkney, took up little space in steamers' holds, and the shipping of livestock was mainly confined to a short season, though in that season it reached enormous proportions. There was, however, one industry which flourished in a spectacular manner at the end of the nineteenth century and the beginning of the twentieth — the herring fishing, which reached its peak in 1905, the record year in which over 1,000,000 barrels of herring were cured in Shetland alone. This involved the movement northwards in early summer of vast quantities of empty barrels (or materials for making them) and the shipping from the islands of vast quantities of cured herring, as well as the movement of hundreds of fish-workers, and there is no doubt that the herring fishing — conducted as it then was in Orkney and in many places throughout Shetland, not least Baltasound — did much to determine the development of transport. One of the great sights of Lerwick's year, down to the 1930s, was the departure, at the end of the herring season in Shetland, of hundreds of girls who had been employed as 'gutters' at the fishing stations, and who, when they left on a steamer for ports further south, were speeded on their way by blasts on the whistles of the many steam drifters in the harbour.

One looks back from 1883, when steamer services had become frequent and reliable, to the infrequent and hazardous transport of the days before steam. Communications by two or three small sailing vessels in a month had been replaced by as many sailings in a week by substantial and powerful steamships which deserved the advertisers' favourite term, 'commodious', at least in comparison with their sail-driven predecessors. It is hardly possible to avoid the conclusion that the coming of steam had meant not only the biggest improvement in transport in the whole history of the islands up to that time, but probably also the most important economic and social revolution which the islands ever experienced, at least before the recent developments associated with oil.

REFERENCES

1 The only significant exceptions have been the following: the extra sailing to Wick which operated most summers from 1892 to 1939 often included Aberdeen on the way north but not on the way south; for many years before 1939 the *Amelia* proceeded direct from Leith to Kirkwall but returned *via* Aberdeen, but later operated direct both north and south; and for some years after 1959 the vessel leaving Leith on Sunday for Orkney proceeded direct to Kirkwall but returned *via* Aberdeen. Christmas and New Year holidays commonly necessitated the omission of Aberdeen from one or two sailings, and when Aberdeen harbour was closed because of the weather a call there sometimes had to be omitted. In the summer of 1964, when there was a typhoid epidemic in Aberdeen, the passenger ships, including the direct boat, worked only from Leith for a week or two.

2 Catherine Sinclair, *Shetland and the Shetlanders* (1840), 72.

3 Christian Ployen, *Reminiscences* (1896), 69-73.

4 A painting of the *Fairy,* displaying the familiar blue-and-white flag which became that of the North of Scotland Company, has been acquired by the Shetland Museum.

5 See Alastair and Anne Cormack, *Days of Orkney Steam.*

6 A 'Shetland Steam Shipping Co.' had been registered on 7 November 1901, but apparently did not operate.

7 I am much indebted to Mr John S. Johnston, Lerwick, for the use of Minute Books of the Company which are in his possession. Other papers of the Company are in the hands of Goodlad and Son, Solicitors, Lerwick. Mr Somner informs me that the *Norseman* was built in 1891 for Mrs M. E. Shaw, Belfast, as the *Minnie Hinde,* was acquired by the Shetland Company in 1905 and was sold to the Bolivian government in 1907. She foundered in 1908. The *Helen* was owned by J. Cameron, Glasgow, and the *Earlford* by George Couper of Helmsdale (1900-05) and Mann, Macneal and Company, Glasgow (1905-15); neither was owned by the Shetland Company.

Chapter Three

THE DEVELOPMENT OF THE MAIN SERVICES
1884 - 1914

In 1883 the main services had taken on a character which was already not dissimilar to the schedule which will be recalled by those whose memories go back to 1939, and the vessels employed bore names which in the main are still familiar today. The outstanding difference between the programme of those days and that of later times was that the time taken between Leith and the islands was shorter. The summer service to Orkney and Shetland was of three sailings weekly, leaving Leith early in the morning on Monday, Wednesday and Friday and each calling at Aberdeen later on the same day. The first of them, the *St Clair,* the west-side boat, reached Stromness on Tuesday morning and Scalloway on Tuesday evening; the second, the *St Magnus,* on the secondary indirect run, reached Kirkwall on Thursday morning and Lerwick on Thursday evening; and the third, the new *St Rognvald,* the 'week-end boat', reached Wick and Kirkwall on Saturday morning and Lerwick on Saturday evening. They were back in Aberdeen on Friday, Saturday and Wednesday respectively. The *St Nicholas,* the Caithness boat, sailed from Leith on Monday evening for Wick and Thurso, returning to Aberdeen and Leith on Friday. But this pattern, which possessed a remarkable symmetry and regularity, was not in fact to be static. Instead, for many years after 1883 there was almost unceasing change, as fresh experiments were made and new services were introduced, and there is no period in the Company's history, except perhaps the pioneering days of the 1830s, when there are so many indications of enterprise.

The manifold changes, year by year, will be recounted in some detail in the following paragraphs, but a brief summary may be given here of the outstanding developments. The call at Wick was dropped from the usual schedule of the 'week-end boat' after 1891, and in its place an extra run to Wick was added, during the height of the summer season, to the programme of the vessel which made the normal run to Wick and

Thurso. Direct sailings between Aberdeen and Lerwick were instituted in the summer of 1891, and they have remained an important feature of the Company's arrangements ever since. Thirdly, a great expansion of tourist traffic led first to cruises to Norway and elsewhere and later to special arrangements for holiday-makers on the Company's normal services and at its hotel at Hillswick; this part of the programme will be described in chapter seven.

The summer programme of 1884 is an outstanding example of diversity, indicating that active experiment was going on. Early in the season, the Caithness boat was leaving Leith on Monday morning for Aberdeen, Wick, Thurso and Stornoway; the secondary indirect boat left on Monday afternoon or evening, calling at Aberdeen, St Margaret's Hope and Scapa on her way to Lerwick; the west-side boat sailed on Wednesday morning or early afternoon and called at Wick as well as her normal ports; and the weekend boat alone adhered to her normal schedule, leaving Leith on Friday morning for Aberdeen, Wick, Kirkwall and Lerwick. In addition, the *Queen,* which at this stage was a kind of 'outside boat', mostly engaged on relief and special duties, was leaving Leith on Wednesday evening or Thursday morning for Fraserburgh, Lerwick and the North Isles of Shetland. Undoubtedly the *Queen's* run and some of the other sailings as well were connected with the opening of the herring fishing season. In July, Wick was dropped from the schedule of the west side run, St Margaret's Hope was transferred from the secondary indirect run to the Caithness run (which no longer extended to Stornoway and now started from Leith on Tuesday), and the *Queen* proceeded to Aberdeen and Wick instead of Fraserburgh before going on to Lerwick and the North Isles. In the later part of the summer season, sailings had reverted to very much what they had been in 1883 — morning departures from Leith for Orkney and Shetland on Monday (west side), Wednesday (Scapa and Lerwick) and Friday (Wick, Kirkwall and Lerwick), and for Caithness on Tuesday; the *Queen* had been withdrawn. In October, Scapa was inserted into the west-side run. During part of the winter the west-side run was dropped.

The summers of 1885, 1886 and 1887 showed less diversity than 1884 had done. Both the west-side run, leaving Leith on Monday morning and returning on Friday, and the weekend run, from Friday to Wednesday, were constant, though in the early summer of 1885 the west-side boat proceeded from the western ports round to Lerwick. The Wick and Thurso run, leaving Leith on Monday afternoon or evening, was extended to Stornoway (every week) until mid-July, and the steamer left Stornoway on Wednesday, returning to Leith on Friday; later in the season St Margaret's Hope was substituted for Stornoway. The secondary indirect run, leaving Leith on Wednesday and returning on Monday, included St Margaret's Hope in the early summer and was extended to the North Isles of Shetland in July, August and September in 1885 and in June as well in 1886. In the winters of 1885-6, 1886-7 and 1887-8, the west-side boat from Leith on Monday morning, while always calling at Stromness, proceeded to Scalloway and to Lerwick in alternate weeks; the Caithness sailing was on Tuesday morning instead of Monday; and Wick was dropped from the schedule of the weekend run.

In the summers from 1888 to 1890 the programme reverted to very much what it had been in 1883. That is, the sailings from Leith, *via* Aberdeen, were as follows:

To Stromness, Scalloway and the west side of Shetland on Monday morning or early afternoon.

To Wick, St Margaret's Hope and Thurso on Tuesday morning or early afternoon.

To Kirkwall and Lerwick on Wednesday morning or early afternoon.

To Wick, Kirkwall and Lerwick on Friday morning or early afternoon.

During the winters of 1888-9, 1889-90 and 1890-91, the Caithness sailing continued to be on Tuesday morning or early afternoon, leaving Aberdeen later the same day; the west-side sailing was on Monday evening from Leith and Tuesday morning from Aberdeen, and in 1888-9 its programme, as in the three previous winters, was the alternation between Lerwick and Scalloway.

The summer of 1891 was again one of experiment. The only run to remain unchanged was, as ever, that to Wick, Kirkwall and Lerwick, leaving Leith on Friday morning. The departure for Wick and Thurso (this year without St Margaret's Hope) was switched to Monday evening, where it was to remain with little change for fifty years, and the west-side run was switched to Tuesday evening. For the first time an attempt was made to separate sailings to Shetland from those to Orkney, for a vessel left Leith for Aberdeen and Kirkwall on Wednesday morning or early afternoon (with St Margaret's Hope in alternate weeks) and also on Saturday, and another left for Aberdeen and Lerwick on Monday evening, while there was an additional run direct from Aberdeen to Lerwick, leaving on Friday about mid-day.

Evidently some of those experiments were not a success, but the direct sailings between Aberdeen and Lerwick had come to stay, and in the summer of 1892 the sailings had taken a new shape, which they retained until 1897. The programme was now as follows:

From Leith via Aberdeen

To Stromness, Scalloway and west side, Monday afternoon or evening in 1892-4, Monday morning 1895-7; returning to Leith on Friday evening.

To Wick and Thurso, Monday afternoon or evening in 1892-4, Monday morning 1895-6; returning to Leith on Thursday evening.

To St Margaret's Hope, Kirkwall and Lerwick, Tuesday evening; returning to Leith on Saturday evening.

To Wick, Thursday night or Friday morning or early afternoon; returning to Leith on Sunday morning.

To Kirkwall and Lerwick, Friday morning or early afternoon; returning to Leith on Wednesday morning.

From Aberdeen

To Lerwick, Monday and Thursday forenoon.

Two minor variations were made in this period: the Monday run to Wick and Thurso was occasionally extended to Stornoway at least in 1894 and 1895; and St Margaret's Hope was dropped from the Tuesday run in 1895. And one major alteration was projected; at the end of 1895, in response to a request for a daily service to Shetland, the Company, pursuing the policy of separating the Shetland sailings from those to Orkney, proposed that Shetland should have four direct sailings from Aberdeen in the week but that the connection between Kirkwall and Lerwick should be eliminated. This proposal was not acceptable, at least in Orkney — a significant commentary on the way in which the pattern of communication to Shetland *via* Orkney, which had come for the first time with the advent of steam navigation, had now become part of the accepted order. A meeting in Lerwick decided to petition the government to finance a daily service in summer and one four times weekly in winter, but this request was rejected.

The institution of the direct run from Aberdeen to Lerwick in the summer of 1891 had given Shetland a fourth summer steamer, and the arrangements made in the summer of 1892 provided a fifth. It was only logical to add another steamer to the two which had previously operated to Shetland in winter. In the winter of 1891-2, therefore, there was a sailing from Leith on Wednesday afternoon or evening, leaving Aberdeen on Thursday morning, for Lerwick direct — in addition to the west-side sailing on Monday (evening 1891-3, morning 1894-8) and the weekend boat. The Caithness service left Leith on Monday morning or early afternoon in 1891-2 and on Tuesday morning in 1893-8. The additional services now being provided to Shetland required new tonnage, and the first *St Giles* was added to the fleet in 1892, for the direct Aberdeen-Lerwick service; the first *St Ninian* followed in 1895, to take over the duties of the paddler *St Magnus,* which was downgraded to a kind of 'outside' boat.

The summers from 1898 to 1905 again form a period during which a pattern persisted with little deviation. The west-side boat adhered to her previous timetable, leaving Leith on Monday morning and arriving at Scalloway on Tuesday afternoon. The secondary indirect boat (which called at St Margaret's Hope in alternate weeks during part of some summers) was stabilised at Tuesday afternoon or evening from Leith, arriving in Lerwick on Thursday — a programme which lasted until 1939. The weekend boat left as usual on Friday morning and arrived at Lerwick on Saturday evening, but had her run extended to Baltasound from 1900 to 1905. The Caithness service left Leith on Monday afternoon or evening. Down to 1902 it included St Margaret's Hope in alternate weeks in the later part of the season, and in the earlier part of the season it included Stornoway at least fortnightly and sometimes Loch Erriboll. In 1898 the Stornoway call was advertised as a weekly one, designed to connect at Stornoway with MacBrayne's steamer to

Oban and Glasgow. In the height of the season there was the additional sailing to Wick on Thursday or Friday morning, but earlier each summer down to 1902 there was a varied schedule for this vessel — Wick, St Margaret's Hope, Stromness and Lerwick in 1898, Wick, St Margaret's Hope, Stromness and Thurso in 1900, 1901 and 1902 — while Loch Erriboll was added to this run to Wick in 1901. The direct sailings from Aberdeen to Lerwick on Monday and Thursday of course continued. The return trips were as follows: from Lerwick on Monday, Tuesday, Thursday and Saturday evenings; from Scalloway on Wednesday evenings; from Kirkwall on Tuesday and Friday mornings; from Stromness on Thursday mornings; from St Margaret's Hope alternate Thursdays; from Thurso on Thursday morning and from Wick on Thursday and Saturday morning. The ships left Aberdeen for Leith as follows: the west-side boat on Thursday night, the Wick boat on Thursday morning and Saturday night, the weekend boat on Tuesday night and the secondary indirect boat on Friday night. The fares from Leith to Lerwick in 1903 were 1st class return £2 12s. and 2nd class return £1 1s.

The winter schedule went on as usual — west-side, Monday morning, Wick and Thurso (with St Margaret's Hope fortnightly and Loch Erriboll occasionally down to 1901) on Tuesday morning, Lerwick direct on Wednesday night and Kirkwall and Lerwick on Friday morning.

The summers from 1906 to 1908 saw very few changes. The additional run to Wick, leaving Leith on Friday morning, was now invariable, without any additional calls, and in 1907 the *Queen* was put on, leaving Leith on Wednesday and Saturday, returning on Monday and Thursday, as a connection from Leith for the direct boat from Aberdeen to Lerwick — an arrangement which pointed forward to the major innovation of 1909, when the vessels on the direct run themselves started from Leith.

In winter there was some experiment. In 1906-7 the run to Wick, Thurso, St Margaret's Hope and Loch Erriboll went on as before, but leaving Leith on Monday morning; in addition to the west-side, direct and weekend runs on their normal time-tables. In 1907-8 and 1908-9, however, there was a Saturday evening sailing from Leith to Scalloway and the west side of Shetland, omitting Stromness; and on Monday night there was a sailing to Stromness and Lerwick. This gave Lerwick three steamers weekly in winter, and Shetland four in all, for the direct run from Leith on Wednesday and the weekend run continued as before.

The years just before the First World War saw steam navigation at its best. The coal-fired triple expansion engine had reached a high pitch of perfection and, although the steam turbine had been coming into use since the beginning of the century, the challenge of the diesel as yet hardly existed. Coal was cheap, labour was cheap, and the speed and regularity of services depended in the long run on how rapidly and efficiently coal could be shovelled into the furnaces. Actual racing between one ship and another was not uncommon, especially among the passenger paddlers on the Firth of Clyde, but it took place also among the pleasure steamers on the Firth of Forth, and one race is recorded between two North of Scotland steamers. In May 1912 the second *St Magnus,* which had recently been launched at Leith by Ramage and Ferguson, was out in the Firth of Forth on her trials and had reached the May Island when she met the *St Rognvald* coming down from Aberdeen. The new steamer ran about three miles past the *St Rognvald,* then turned and challenged her to a race. The *St Magnus* gradually gained on the older ship, but, when within half a mile of her, the master saw he could not reach the pier-heads first, so he ran up towards the Forth Bridge to work off his surplus steam, leaving the *St Rognvald* to enter Leith.

It was in this period (from 1909 to 1914 to be precise) that the shipping company provided the best service the islands have ever had. In summer, Shetland had a steamer from Leith and Aberdeen five times a week, Orkney had three and Caithness two. On Monday morning (or occasionally Sunday evening), the west-side boat left Leith for Stromness, Scalloway, Walls and Hillswick, with fortnightly calls at Spiggie, Voe, Brae and Aith. On Monday evening the Caithness boat sailed for Wick and Thurso, calling at St Margaret's Hope in alternate weeks, and she sailed again for Wick alone on Friday morning. On Tuesday afternoon and Friday morning there were sailings to Kirkwall and Lerwick. And on Wednesday evening and Saturday evening a 'direct boat' sailed from Leith for Aberdeen and Lerwick. From Leith to Aberdeen there were seven sailings in the week.

One reason for this lavish provision was that the *St Sunniva* had been withdrawn from the cruises after 1908, and became available for the direct run, so that the *St Giles* (II) and she each made a return run every week from Leith to Aberdeen and Lerwick. The development of the direct run had been a remarkable feature. In its early days the small *St Giles,* of only 407 tons, had sufficed; the second *St Giles,* of 609 tons, had taken her place; and in 1913 the *St Sunniva* (864 tons) and *St Margaret* (943 tons) were operating the service. It had proved a successful innovation.

The Company was uncommonly well supplied with ships at this point, and possessed a more up-to-date fleet than it was to have again for a long time. At the outbreak of the First World War the fleet included the *St Margaret,* built in 1913 to replace the *St Giles* (II), which herself had been built only in 1903, the *St Magnus* (II), of 1912, the *St Rognvald* (II), of 1901, the *St Ninian* (1895) and the *St Sunniva* (1887). Of the main-service ships, only the *St Clair,* already forty-six years old, could have been called a veteran. There had for some years always been a ship on the active list but in reserve, and the loss of the second oldest of the main line fleet, the *St Nicholas* (1871), in June 1914, did not embarrass the Company. The total tonnage, before the loss of the *St Nicholas,* was a little over 6,000.

The considerable summer-time expansion was obviously mainly in the interests of the growing passenger traffic, and the winter time-table retained the shape it had taken in 1907-8, giving Shetland four calls in the week. That is, a boat left Leith on Saturday evening for Scalloway, Walls and Hillswick, alternating fortnightly between a call at Brae and calls at Voe and Aith. On Monday evening there was a sailing to Stromness and Lerwick and on the same evening the Caithness boat left for Wick and Thurso, with fortnightly calls at St Margaret's Hope and an occasional call at Loch Erriboll. The direct sailing to Aberdeen and Lerwick on Wednesday and the Kirkwall and Lerwick sailing on Friday morning continued as in summer. In the winter following the outbreak of war in August 1914 the direct run was dropped, the west-side run included Stromness and there was a Tuesday sailing from Leith for Kirkwall and Lerwick as in summer.

Chapter Four

THE MAIN SERVICES BETWEEN THE
FIRST WORLD WAR AND 1966

Immediately after the First War, the Company was hampered by the serious depletion of its fleet. The loss of the *St Nicholas* in 1914 had never been made good, the two newest ships, the *St Magnus* and the *St Margaret,* had both been lost during the war and had not been replaced, and some time elapsed before the *St Ninian* was refitted after her war service on the Pentland Firth. In the war years, when the Company's vessels had been called on for many duties outwith their normal services, some purely cargo vessels had been acquired for the first time, and they made it possible to maintain the essential transport of goods.

Throughout the summer of 1919, however, the passenger services were greatly curtailed: neither the Caithness service nor the secondary indirect service could be operated, leaving only the west-side service, a direct boat leaving Leith on Monday afternoon or evening and the invariable weekend boat. In the following winter, the *St Ninian* had returned to duty, but the services continued as in summer, except that the direct boat sailed from Leith on Wednesday afternoon or evening. By the summer of 1920, there was a partial replacement of the war casualties, for MacBrayne's *Chieftain* was acquired, to become the *St Margaret* (II), and she was assigned to the west-side service, leaving a vessel available for the secondary indirect service from Leith on Tuesday afternoon or evening. Even in this summer, however, the Caithness service was not fully restored, and the fleet was still one less in number (of passenger ships) than it had been in August 1914. The service which in the long run suffered permanently as a result of the depletion of the fleet was the direct service, for which only one vessel, the *St Sunniva,* was now available. In the summer of 1919, as already mentioned, she left Leith for Aberdeen and Lerwick on Monday

5. *St Nicholas*

6. *St Rognvald (I)* in her original state

7. *St Rognvald (I)* as reconstructed for cruising

8. *St Sunniva (I)* as yacht

9. *St Sunniva (I)* ashore in Orkney, 1914

10. *Norseman*

afternoon and evening and made only one trip in the week. In the summer of 1920 she was making two runs each week from Aberdeen to Lerwick, but was not touching Leith at all. Thereafter she settled down into what remained the summer schedule until 1939: from Leith on Monday morning, leaving Aberdeen in the evening for Lerwick, from Lerwick on Wednesday at noon for Aberdeen, from Aberdeen on Thursday at 2 p.m. for Lerwick and from Lerwick on Saturday at 5 p.m. for Aberdeen and Leith. In winter she left Leith at first on Wednesday, later on Tuesday, afternoon or evening, and Aberdeen on Wednesday morning, and left Lerwick on Friday at 4 p.m. In the summer of 1919 the times of departure from Leith of the west-side boat and the weekend boat were put back from Monday morning and Friday morning to Sunday and Thursday afternoon or evening, where they afterwards remained (except for an experiment in deferring the west side sailing to Monday evening in the winter of 1919-20 and the summer and autumn of 1920). The advancement of the sailing hour from Leith by approximately twelve hours, without any corresponding change in the time of arrival at the other end of the trip, was typical of the general slowing down of the services at this period. Possibly the increasing cost of coal — and, indeed, the scarcity of coal during the repeated coal strikes — necessitated the reduction of speeds at sea and in fact no voyages made between the wars equalled the records set up before 1914. But the loss of time arose mainly from the increased number of hours spent idle in Aberdeen on the way north by every vessel except the direct boat. Thus, a ship on one of the indirect runs, leaving Leith at any time from noon onwards, loitered her way to Aberdeen and did not leave there until 11 a.m. (altered in the 1930s to 12 noon) the following day. With a call at Kirkwall or Stromness, she was not in Lerwick or Scalloway until forty-eight hours or more after her departure from Leith. On the southward run, however, the sailing times were such that the total time taken did not exceed thirty-six hours. The passage between Aberdeen and Orkney and *vice versa* was never an overnight passage except on the southward run of the secondary indirect boat.

After 1920 the whole programme was stabilised on a pattern which continued until 1939. The sailings from Leith (*via* Aberdeen) were as follows:

D

Summer[1]

Sunday afternoon or evening	Stromness, Scalloway and west side.
Monday morning or early afternoon	Lerwick.
Monday afternoon or evening	Wick, Thurso (and St Margaret's Hope fortnightly).
Tuesday afternoon or evening	Kirkwall and Lerwick.
Thursday afternoon or evening	Kirkwall and Lerwick.
Friday morning	Wick

In addition, there was a direct run from Aberdeen to Lerwick on Thursday at 2 p.m.

Returning south as follows:—

From Lerwick *via* Kirkwall	Monday, 5 p.m. Friday, 4 a.m. (later 2 a.m.)
From Lerwick to Aberdeen	Wednesday, noon. Saturday, 5 p.m.
From Scalloway	Wednesday, 6 p.m.
From Kirkwall	Tuesday, 6 a.m. Friday, 5 p.m.
From Stromness	Thursday morning.
From Aberdeen	Tuesday evening. Thursday morning (July-August). Thursday evening. Friday morning (June, September). Saturday morning. Sunday morning.

The Caithness boat returned from Wick direct to Leith on Saturday evening.

Winter

Sunday afternoon or evening	Stromness, Scalloway and west side.
Monday afternoon or evening	Wick, Thurso (St Margaret's Hope fortnightly).
Tuesday afternoon or evening	Lerwick.
Thursday afternoon or evening	Kirkwall and Lerwick.

Returning south as follows:—

From Lerwick *via* Kirkwall	Monday, 5 p.m.
From Lerwick to Aberdeen	Friday, 4 p.m.
From Scalloway	Wednesday, 6 p.m.
From Kirkwall	Tuesday, 6 a.m.
From Stromness	Thursday morning.
From Aberdeen	Tuesday evening. Thursday evening. Friday morning. Saturday morning.

During this period some important changes were made in the fleet. The *St Magnus* (III) appeared in 1924 to supersede the *St Margaret* (II); after the first *St Sunniva* was lost in 1930 she was replaced within little over a year by the second, and in 1937 the Company at last parted with the old *St Clair* and introduced a second ship of that name. The *St Clement,* a cargo ship with accommodation for twelve passengers, was built in 1928. The changes were not adequate to make the fleet as up-to-date as it had been in 1914, for in 1939 it still included the *St Ninian* of 1895 and the *St Rognvald* of 1900, as well as the *Earl of Zetland* (1877) and the *St Ola* (1892). But the new passenger vessels were much larger than those in the pre-1914 fleet, and by 1939 the total tonnage had reached 8,000. The additional tonnage was, however, mainly for the accommodation of passengers in summer. It was not altogether a novelty to lay up ships in winter, for the *St Sunniva* (I) had been mainly a summer-time ship in her cruising days and the second *St Rognvald* had been little used in winter when she was new. But this policy was now pursued more emphatically than before. For many years the *St Magnus* (III) and the *St Sunniva* (II) were both laid up for all but the summer months, and the *St Ninian,* too, was little used except in summer; the *St Catherine,* on the other hand, acquired in 1930 after the loss of the *St Sunniva* (I), operated only in winter after her first season. It was a further economy that several of the ships — the *St Ninian, St Rognvald* (II) and *St Magnus* (III) — were so designed that a very large part of the passenger accommodation could be sealed off, with consequent reduction in registered tonnage; for example, the *St Ninian* was rated at 393 tons in summer and 284 tons in winter. The predominantly slow rate of steaming — seldom exceeding 11 knots — represented a saving in coal.

It says much for the economy and efficiency with which the Company managed its affairs — though no doubt it also reflects increased traffic — that in the 1930s there was a reduction of approximately 10 per cent in charges. The first class return fare from Leith to Lerwick was reduced from £3 16s. 6d. to £3 9s., and from Aberdeen to Lerwick from £3 6s. 6d. to £3.

The competition of air transport made its appearance in the years before the Second World War. After some experimental flights, services to and from Orkney were established in 1933, and for a time private enterprise even provided services among the Orkney Islands which British European Airways later abandoned. An air service to Shetland started in the summer of 1936 — exactly a century after the first steamship service — but the first air mail to the islands was at the end of January 1937, at a time when a prolonged series of severe gales had caused unparalleled dislocation of the steamer services. It happened that all the passenger ships in service reached Shetland but were stormbound there. The *St Ninian* reached Scalloway on Wednesday, 20 January, and proceeded to Aith, returning to Scalloway on Saturday and remaining there until the following Friday. The *St Catherine,* on her passage north from Aberdeen on Wednesday the 20th, had to heave-to south of Fair Isle, and was thirty hours on her passage: she then had to lie in the harbour for more than twenty-four hours (while a trawler took off her passengers), and did not berth at Victoria Pier until Friday night, 22 January. There she remained for five days, breaking a succession of hawsers even although for part of the time she was steaming to ease the strain and keep her off the pier; on Wednesday, 27 January, she anchored in the harbour. The *St Magnus,* leaving Aberdeen on Saturday, 23 January, had to lie at Kirkwall until Wednesday and came alongside Victoria Pier on Thursday. No ship left Shetland between Tuesday, 19 January, and Friday, 29 January, and when all three did leave, on the 29th, Aberdeen Harbour was closed and they had to proceed to Leith. The *St Fergus* left Leith on 18 January for Stromness and returned on 2 February and the *St Clement* left Leith on 18 January for the Caithness run and returned on 3 February. Thus, when the weather first moderated, there was no vessel available at Aberdeen to convey mails north, and in those circumstances the Post Office chartered a plane to carry letter mail from Aberdeen to Shetland on Friday, 30 January. It was not until November 1937 that a regular air mail service to Shetland began. It is somewhat ironical that the first air mail, in 1937, was organised in the circumstances then obtaining, for in the years after the Second World War experience was quite contrary: the larger and more powerful ships, with new navigational aids, could be relied on to get through when the planes were grounded, and it became a common occurrence for would-be air passengers to have to transfer to the ships. The saying in Lerwick was, 'If you want to get there, go by the *St Clair'.*

The Second War, like the first, made heavy demands on the Company. The *St Sunniva* (II), commandeered at the outbreak of war, later became a rescue ship and was lost while on that service. The *St Magnus* was requisitioned for a time, but in the summer of 1940 was released in return for the *St Clair* (II). To replace requisitioned tonnage, the Company acquired the *Highlander* and re-named her *St Catherine* (II), but her career with the Company was short before she was torpedoed. The *St Clement* and *St Fergus* were also lost, one by enemy action, the other in collision. The *St Ninian* returned to her old station on the Pentland Firth, and served there in company with the *Earl of Zetland* (II). The only two vessels of the peace-time fleet which were latterly available for the main services were the *St Magnus,* which operated from Aberdeen to Lerwick, and the *St. Rognvald,* which operated from Aberdeen to Kirkwall. Various vessels carried on a cargo service from Leith.

Details of the war-time careers of the various ships, with

episodes heroic and tragic, are given in Part II, but something may be said here of 'the day-to-day story of all kinds of traffic safely conveyed to and from the islands of Orkney and Shetland during these six years of total war. Altogether, about sixty vessels were at various times under the Company's management and control, carrying troops, civilians, general cargo, livestock and His Majesty's Mails. Widely varied was the cargo handled in the general trade to Orkney and Shetland, amounting to about half a million tons; from guns, explosives and ammunition to vegetables, ice, clothing, hardware, fruit, groceries, fish, wool and dozens of other commodities, including ropes, manures, tractors, machinery, motor cars, vans and ambulances, with as many as 2,000 individual consignments in a single cargo. Indeed a mixed bag, from the means of dealing death to the necessities of maintaining life. During the six years, apart from trooping, over 300,000 passengers were conveyed by the Company's own vessels, including service men and women, as well as civilians permitted to travel. These islands were, of course, "Protected Areas", and ordinary travellers were not allowed to enter or leave without permission. As for livestock, an important part of the Company's work, 176,000 sheep, 35,000 cattle, 4,500 pigs and 3,000 horses were transported over the period; as well as 1,300,000 packages of H.M. Mails. In the course of these sailings, the Company's vessels completed 1,600 voyages, in addition to 1,800 trips across the Pentland Firth and 900 inter-island voyages in the North Isles of Shetland, steaming about 840,000 miles — a distance equal to more than thirty-three times round the world. With such importance did the Authorities regard the maintenance of the service to the islands, the safe transit of foodstuffs, war material and Service personnel and passengers, that — during the later years of the war — special naval escort vessels, equipped with radar, were provided, notwithstanding the scarcity and many duties of this type of craft. The whole management and administration were directed towards providing the best possible service and in spite of losses suffered and the dangers and risks endured, the Company is quietly proud of the fact that the needs of the Island Communities were faithfully met, under war conditions. Orkney and Shetland, cut off geographically from the Mainland, were not cut off by sea, in spite of determined enemy efforts'.[2]

At the end of the war, the St Clair, St Ninian and Earl of

Zetland (II) returned safely from their war service, but the Company was short of one major ship, owing to the loss of the *St Sunniva,* and the *St Ninian,* already fifty years old, was not brought back into peace-time service. It was obvious that the *St Rognvald,* built in 1901, was also nearing the end of her useful life.

Services had therefore to be drastically reduced and the whole schedule largely re-cast. The west-side service was not resumed, the weekend boat (the aged *St Rognvald*) went no further north than Kirkwall and the direct boat no longer proceeded to Leith. A sailing from Leith by the *St Magnus* on Monday afternoon or evening to Aberdeen, Kirkwall and Lerwick, returning on Saturday evening, was a modification of the old secondary indirect run but now became the primary (indeed for a time the only) indirect service. The *Amelia* helped to overtake Orkney cargo needs. The direct boat, the *St Clair* (II), left Aberdeen on Monday and Thursday, usually at 5 p.m., leaving Lerwick on Tuesday and Saturday at 5 p.m., but no longer touched Leith at all. The schedule was the same in winter as in summer. The Caithness service was resumed in 1950 by cargo vessels, and ceased altogether in 1956. Calls at St Margaret's Hope continued until 1966.

In 1950, when the new *St Ninian* was added to the fleet and took over the primary indirect service, there was some improvement. The *St Magnus* was available as the weekend boat, and in the summer months (mid-May to mid-September) her programme was extended to Lerwick as in earlier times. The old *St Rognvald,* in her last summer, was restored to a truncated west-side service, for she left Leith, as of old, on Sunday afternoon or evening for Aberdeen and Stromness (and St Margaret's Hope fortnightly), but there was no extension to Scalloway. When the new *St Rognvald* (III) came on in 1955, she was detailed for a service leaving Leith on Sunday evening or early Monday morning for Kirkwall, thence Stromness, and she made some calls at Scrabster in connection with the erection of the nuclear power-station at Dounreay. Her advent made the *Amelia* redundant. One minor change in this period was the cessation of calls at Fair Isle: until 1950 vessels on the Kirkwall-Lerwick run called by prior arrangement off the island to uplift or set down passengers, who were boated to and from the shore.

After the Second War, the Company had to face very

changed working conditions among dockers and shore staff
generally — and it is sometimes forgotten that the cost of shore
labour accounts for a very large proportion of a shipping company's total expenditure. It was no longer economic, or even
possible, to call on a labour force for brief periods outside
the ordinary working day, and certain changes had to be made
in the time-tables in order to make full use of dock and other
labour during the normal working hours, and also to meet the
convenience of the staffs of shippers. The consequence was a
still further slowing-down of the schedule of the indirect
services, now on the southward trip as well. Going north, the
vessels leaving Leith on Monday and Thursday evenings did not
leave Aberdeen until the following evening and Kirkwall until
noon or later on the third day: their times of leaving Leith,
however, were usually later than they had been in the 1930s, and
the total length of the voyage was still approximately forty-eight
hours. (Beginning in 1960, the weekend boat was posted for
12 noon from Aberdeen on Fridays in July and August, giving a
daylight trip to Kirkwall.) On the southward run, the time of
leaving Lerwick was Sunday night instead of Monday evening
and Thursday night instead of Friday morning, with arrivals at
Leith on Tuesday and Saturday evenings, so that the pre-war
thirty-six hours was now extended to nearly forty-eight. The
increasing emphasis on overnight passages, while an economic
necessity and undoubtedly time-saving for travellers on business,
represented a real loss to those who travelled for pleasure;
many people must have happy memories of the daylight passage
from Orkney to Aberdeen, when the ship left Kirkwall on
Tuesday at 6 a.m. It was perhaps some compensation for the
slowing-up of the time-table that, by a revolution in practice,
the posted times of sailing were now in general adhered to.
Previously the lateness of departure, especially from Leith and
Aberdeen, had been notorious: two or two and a half hours
after the posted time was quite usual, and even when there was
no cause for delay a matter of ten minutes' grace was always
allowed. It was said during the First World War that the
German submarines knew the posted times of sailing but always
missed the ship because, after a long wait, they concluded that
she had passed. Since the Second World War, however, it has
become almost a point of honour to cast off on the stroke of the
hour, and passengers are deprived of the scope for speculation

which used to be provided by the ringing of the bells and the awaited arrival of the mails (which were always taken aboard last). It is also true that, with the substitution of oil fuel for coal in the remaining steamships and the general superseding of steamers by motor vessels, the time actually on passage was reduced, especially on the direct run. The second *St Clair* commonly did this run in fourteen or fourteen-and-a-half hours, against the sixteen hours which were more usual before the War, and the third *St Clair* did it in twelve.

Despite all competition, and changes in the pattern of communications, the Company's trade showed substantial increases as compared with the figures for 1938. The number of trips made by passengers increased by 50% — from 50,906 in 1938 to 75,586 in 1961, and the figure for 1965 was still slightly higher than the 1961 figure. The tonnage of goods carried doubled over the same period — 51,876 tons in 1938, 66,920 in 1948, 103,126 in 1961 and about 109,000 in 1965. The principal imports to the islands had come to be feeding-stuffs and fertilisers. The tonnage of the former was 12,359 in 1938 (but this included traffic between Leith and Aberdeen, which came to an end after the War), 8,217 in 1948 and 24,093 in 1961; and the latter increased spectacularly from a mere 431 tons in 1938 to 6,804 tons in 1961. The exports from the islands fluctuated, but in general showed increases too: eggs from 1,650 tons in 1938 to a peak of 4,321 tons in 1961, whisky from 1,490 to 2,600 tons, fresh fish from 1,869 tons to a peak of 4,400 tons in 1965, while frozen fish (a novel commodity) accounted for 2,600 tons in 1965. Besides, there were enormous numbers of livestock: sheep increased from 66,513 in 1938 to a peak of almost 100,000 in 1961 and cattle from 10,483 in 1938 to 23,000 in 1965.

While the number of ships was again reduced — from nine in 1939 to seven in 1966 — it was possible to carry the increased traffic because the tonnage of the fleet once more increased, to 9,000 tons, against 8,000 tons in 1939 and 6,000 tons in 1914. Of all the changes after the Second War, none impressed the passenger more than the increased size of the ships. When one travelled, as I did from Shetland in 1931, in the first *St Clair*, of only 600 tons, I would not have believed that within thirty years I would travel in a third *St Clair*, of 3,000 tons.

REFERENCES

1 June-September inclusive, except the additional run to Wick, which operated only in July and August.
2 Extracted from *A Northern Saga: Chronicle of the North of Scotland & Orkney & Shetland Steam Navigation Co., Ltd., during the Second World War,* issued by the Company in 1946.

Chapter Five

THE PENTLAND FIRTH AND THE NORTH ISLES OF ORKNEY[1]

The early arrangements by which the Orkney mail was conveyed across the Pentland Firth, after the mail coach had brought it to Thurso, were described in Chapter 1, and there was little change until the middle of the nineteenth century. The possibility of using a steamship on the crossing was considered as early at least as 1843, but the obstacle for steamships, as it had been for a larger sailing vessel, was the lack of a pier or harbour on the Caithness side. The construction of a pier at Scrabster, two miles from Thurso, altered the situation. It was presumably in existence in 1852, when the vessel serving Wick from Leith and Aberdeen had her run extended to Thurso.

John Stanger, a Stromness shipbuilder, obtained the contract for the carriage of the mail from Scrabster to Stromness, and in 1856 built a small wooden paddle steamer, the *Royal Mail,* of 103 gross tons, which began daily sailings in April 1856 and continued until the end of March 1868. Stanger had originally fitted her as a schooner, so that she could sail to the Tyne and have her engine installed, and after he sold her to an Aberdeen firm she had her engine removed and was wrecked on her first voyage for her new owners.

When a change took place, the initiative again came from Orkney. George Robertson (1832-1916), a native of South Ronaldsay but brought up in Stronsay, had, in the course of his career as a master mariner in the Mediterranean, done a good deal of profitable salvage work. From his savings he was able in 1863 to buy a small wooden screw steamer, the *Quarry Maid,* which he renamed the *Orcadia.* She was 83 feet in length and 20 feet of beam, and her gross tonnage was 101. This vessel inaugurated a steam service between Kirkwall and the North Isles of Orkney, making her first official trip, from Sanday, Stronsay and Eday to Kirkwall, at the beginning of April 1865.[2]

Previously there had been no regular service at all, for passengers and mails alike had been conveyed in small sailing vessels which were at the mercy of the weather and whose schedules were liable to interruption owing to the vicissitudes of cargo requirements. Now, however, passengers were conveyed in what was considered great comfort — thirty people could sit in the first *Orcadia's* cabin — and at what was thought great speed — the vessel did eight knots. Not only did the service appeal to islesmen on their necessary occasions, but townsmen patronised the *Orcadia* for pleasure, and in her very first year an excursion to Fair Isle was planned, but it had to be abandoned because of unfavourable weather. (This pioneering venture was an example followed by the second and third *Orcadias,* both of which have cruised to Fair Isle.) From almost the beginning of the service, the *Orcadia* was assisted by a small paddler, the *Rover.* At the end of 1867 the Orkney Steam Navigation Company was formed, with Robertson as managing director, and the original *Orcadia* was replaced in May 1868 by a new vessel of the same name, specially built at South Shields for the service.

Stimulated by these successes, Robertson next obtained the contract for the Scrabster-Stromness service, and, after briefly using the *Wellington* and the *Pera,* in 1869 he placed the new screw steamer *Express* on this service. The *Express* was to have a long life, of which some account is given in Part II of this book, but her career on the Pentland Firth was comparatively short.

The railway had meantime been pushing further north, stage by stage, until in 1874 it reached Thurso. The Railway Company, following the policy pursued by railways elsewhere in Britain, decided to run a steamer from its terminus on the mainland, and when the mail contract came up for renewal in 1877 it was acquired by the railway company. The railway steamer *John o' Groat* came into service on the Pentland Firth on 27 July 1877. This vessel, of 384 gross tons, was built at Dundee and had a compound engine of 115 h.p. After five years' service on the Pentland Firth she passed through various hands until she was wrecked in the Adriatic in 1892.

The phase of railway management, however, was a brief one, for in 1882 the Pentland Firth service was handed over to the North of Scotland Company, which replaced the *John o' Groat* by the *St Olaf.* The vessel evidently proved unsatisfactory, for she was sold in 1890, and in 1892 the service was taken over by the *St Ola* (I), which was to serve for fifty-nine years.

The new vessel was of 231 tons gross, as against the *St Olaf's* 205, but she had a triple expansion engine of 105 h.p., as against the *St Olaf's* compound engine of only 65, and this gave her the power and reserve of speed necessary to maintain the service in those tide-swept waters. Her long service received recognition in 1937, when she was invited to be present at the Coronation Review, but the Company found it impossible to release her.

In the interval between the sale of the *St Olaf* and the introduction of the *St Ola,* the *John o' Groat* served briefly once more, and so did the *Express;* the *Argyll* was chartered for a time from the Argyll Steam Ship Company of Glasgow, and the *Queen* also did two spells of duty. During the First World War, the *St Ninian* supplemented the *St Ola* by maintaining a service between Scrabster and Longhope, and in the Second War both the *Earl of Zetland* (II) and the *St Ninian* were on the Pentland Firth. For many years the *St Ola* (I) and her successor were relieved when they went for overhaul by the *Earl of Zetland* (I and II), and later the *St Clement* (II) became the usual relief ship.

Partly because the Pentland Firth service had been initiated by a Stromness owner, but partly also because Stromness, the second town in Orkney, had a better harbour than Scrabster, Stromness was from the beginning the headquarters of the Pentland Firth steamer, and so it has remained. The precise times of sailing have been modified throughout the generations, sometimes in accordance with the time-table of the trains to and from Thurso. For example, in 1883 the crossing was made at night; in 1898, while the time of departure from Stromness had become 9.40 a.m., the return trip from Scrabster was not until 5 p.m.; in 1908 the ship left Scrabster about 4 p.m. and was due in Scapa about 6.50 p.m. and Stromness at 8.30 p.m.; for many years now the departure from Stromness has been about 9 a.m. and the ship has left Scrabster on the return trip at or about mid-day, which gives time for a second trip if necessary. Until the Second War, the vessel, after leaving Stromness, called at the pier at Scapa where the main mail was taken on board, and also called off Hoxa, South Ronaldsay, on her way to Scrabster. On the return trip she likewise delivered the mail at Scapa, but a call at Hoxa was not normal. After the Second War, the intermediate calls were discontinued, so that the vessel could

now normally make a smarter, direct run between Stromness and
Scrabster, passing the magnificent cliffs of the west side of Hoy,
which surely make this the most spectacular short sea trip in
the British Isles.

With the advent of an air service to Orkney in the 1930s,
first-class mail started to go by air, so that the importance of
the *St Ola* was reduced, and many passengers preferred an air
journey to the long and tedious journey by train to and from
Thurso and a sea crossing which many dreaded and for which the
first *St Ola* offered few amenities. Despite the appearance in 1951
of the second *St Ola,* a much larger vessel with vastly superior
accommodation, it might well have seemed that the Pentland
Firth route would become of less than secondary importance
in the pattern of communications. However, the development of
road travel in private cars gave the old route a new lease
of life and made it busier than ever in the tourist season.
A Sunday service was introduced for the first time in 1959, and
it became quite common in the height of the season for the
St Ola to have to make a double crossing to keep up with the
constant flow of cars, while from time to time another vessel
took the 'overflow' of cars. In 1965 it became apparent that
even this was not enough, and the *St Clement* was put on the
passage in the peak period to supplement the *St Ola.* The
number of cars carried in 1938 was negligible, and even ten years
later, in the last days of the first *St Ola,* it was only 286, but
in 1961 the figure had risen to 4,638, in 1965 to 5,350 and in
1974 (the last year of the second *St Ola*) to no less than 9500.

Even the second *St Ola,* however, operated the old 'lift on,
lift off' system for vehicles, hoisting them by her derrick, and
experience in many other parts of the world showed that the
growing demand could ultimately be met only by a ship with
bow and stern loading, where cars drove aboard on to a car
deck and drove off at the other end. Consequently, as part of
a general re-shaping of the services (which will be dealt with
in its context in chapter 8), a third *St Ola* was introduced in
January 1975. A vessel of 1345 gross tons, specially designed
for the work, she can carry over ninety cars and accommodate
400 passengers (all of whom can be seated under cover — a
change from the seating for 30 in the first *Orcadia's* cabin). Her
twin-screw machinery gives her a speed of 15 knots and reduces
the time on passage to two hours. Bow-thrust units provide

the necessary manoeuvrability at the loading ramps at the ports
and she has fin-stabilisers. Her somewhat stumpy appearance
conceals a length of 230 feet, similar to that of the main-service
ships of two generations ago, with their slender hulls and vastly
different profiles. The new vessel's success can be measured by
a further vast increase in the number of vehicles carried, to over
15,000 in 1976.

The services from Kirkwall to the North Isles of Orkney
were maintained principally by the second *Orcadia,* built in
1868, for over sixty years. Originally 120 feet in length, with
an engine of 60 h.p., she was lengthened by 20 feet in 1884.
The *Express,* which returned briefly to the Pentland Firth
crossing in 1890-1, was occupied mainly in carrying general
cargo between Kirkwall and Scottish east coast ports. The
Orkney Steam Navigation Company purchased a small iron screw
steamer, the *Fawn,* of 82 tons, in 1892 to supplement the
Orcadia on the North Isles run; she had been built in 1869 and
she served until 1917, when she was sold. She was succeeded by
the *Countess of Bantry,* an iron screw steamer of 90 tons, built
at Belfast in 1884; this vessel was acquired in 1919 and sold
in 1928. The Company also owned from 1892 to 1899 a wooden
smack, the *Cock of the North,* of 60 tons, built at Aberdeen
in 1835 and apparently owned for a time by the Aberdeen, Leith
and Clyde.

Two new steamers were provided for the North Isles between the Wars — the *Earl Thorfinn* in 1928 and the *Earl Sigurd*
in 1931, of 345 and 221 gross tons respectively. Only in 1931,
when the *Sigurd* arrived, was the veteran *Orcadia* withdrawn
from service, but she was not broken up until 1934. The two
Earls, which turned out to be the last steamers in the service,
served the islands before, during and after the Second World
War and earned the respect not only of islanders but of visiting
tourists who took advantage of the opportunities they offered
for round trips. Those who knew them well can recount many
adventures, but the one episode which deserves never to be
forgotten was the voyage of the *Earl Thorfinn* in the great
storm of 31 January 1953, which caused the loss of the *Princess
Victoria,* with 133 lives, in the North Channel and devastated
whole tracts of territory throughout the length and breadth of
Scotland. The *Thorfinn* left Stronsay that morning for Sanday
and finished up in Aberdeen, driven by a 100 mile an hour

gale which gave the master no chance to do anything but run
before it. She suffered much damage on deck, which was
virtually stripped of all movable gear, and it is creditable both
to her sturdiness and to the seamanship of her company that
she survived, after being given up for lost.

A critical situation arose some years after World War II.
Both the *Thorfinn* and the *Sigurd,* being coal-burning steamers,
were outmoded and increasingly uneconomic to run, but the
Orkney Steam Navigation Company lacked the resources to
replace them, in view of the sharp rise in the cost of new
tonnage. In 1960 the Highlands and Islands Shipping Service
Act made provision for government assistance to be applied
to shipping in the western and northern isles, but even so neither
the Orkney Steam nor the North of Scotland was prepared
to undertake the maintenance of the North Isles service. A
new company was therefore formed, the Orkney Islands
Shipping Company, with two government-appointed directors
as chairman and vice-chairman. This new company took over
the assets of the Orkney Steam Navigation Company (including
its two steamers) and chartered from the Secretary of State
for Scotland the motor ship *Orcadia* (III), of 896 tons, which
had been built at Aberdeen for the service and arrived at
Kirkwall on 30 June 1962. The *Earl Thorfinn* was sent to be
broken up in February 1963, and the *Earl Sigurd* was retained
as a subsidiary to the *Orcadia* until July 1969, when she followed
her former consort to Bo'ness. The third *Orcadia* was a vastly
superior vessel in every way to her predecessors, but the inroads
made on passenger traffic among the islands by the aeroplanes
limited even her utility for passengers, and the replacement
for the *Earl Sigurd* was the *Islander,* a vessel of 250 gross tons
carrying only twelve passengers.

The problem of services between the Mainland and the
other islands has always been a more complex one in Orkney
than in Shetland, where the more important islands are close
to the Mainland and several of them lie in such a position
that they can be easily reached by a single direct route up the
east coast from Lerwick. In Orkney, by contrast, the North
Isles are more scattered and some of them far from the
Mainland, and there are also the South Isles, with their quite
separate needs. Consequently, the service provided by successive
Orcadias and other steamers of the Orkney Steam Navigation

11. *St Catherine (I) as Olive*

13. *St Rognvald (II)*

Company had to be supplemented. The normal North Isles steamer routes at first served only Stronsay, Eday, Sanday, Westray and Papa Westray, usually three times a week, and North Ronaldsay once a week or at times less frequently. A separate service was required for Gairsay, Wyre, Egilsay and Rousay, and a little steamer, the *Lizzie Burroughs,* based on Rousay, attended to their needs from 1879 until 1892, when the Orkney Steam began to serve those islands. Shapinsay, so close to Kirkwall, qualified for a boat of its own and a daily service, and this was given by the *Iona* from 1893 to 1964, then by the *Klydon* (1963-9) and the *Clytus* (from 1970).

In the south of the island group, ferries linked Burray with the Mainland and South Ronaldsay with Burray, while the *St Ola* made calls at Hoxa until the Second War and the westside and Caithness boats called at St Margaret's Hope; North of Scotland boats continued to call at St Margaret's Hope until 1966. But after the Second War the Churchill Barriers provided a continuous roadway to South Ronaldsay and Burray. Hoy, along with Graemsay and Flotta, had and has a boat of its own, based on Stromness: the *Saga* from 1893 to 1895, the first *Hoy Head,* another of those long-serving steamers, from 1896 to 1956, and a second *Hoy Head,* a motor vessel, from 1958. Each of those lesser services has had its devotees, and each has its own story.

REFERENCES

1 This chapter makes no attempt to compete with the very full account given by Alastair and Anne Cormack, *Days of Orkney Steam.* In originally compiling my own account, I owed a great deal to the researches of Mr Graeme Somner, published in 'The Pentland Firth Mail Service' (*Marine News,* xvii, 316-9), 'Pioneer of Steam in the Orkneys' (*Sea Breezes,* xxxix, 85-8) and 'George Robertson, Kirkwall' (*Marine News,* xix, 313-7) and to those of the late Mr Ernest Marwick, who wrote on 'The First North Isles Steamer' in *The Orcadian* of 1 April 1965. Both Mr Somner and Mr Marwick supplied me with further information. The former discovered an earlier Orcadian steamer — the *Northman,* built by Denny of Dumbarton in 1847 for the Kirkwall Steam Navigation Company and sold in 1851 to A. A. Laird, Glasgow. It seems that as early as 1860 the Aberdeen, Leith and Clyde Company considered putting on a steamer in the North Isles of Orkney, but decided against it.

2 The year has often been given as 1864, but the evidence of newspaper reports is conclusive for 1865.

E

Chapter Six

THE NORTH ISLES OF SHETLAND

As was shown in the first chapter, there were generations during which trade flowed directly between each little Shetland 'port' and either the continent or Britain, and as long as this was so there was little incentive to develop internal communications within Shetland. The emergence of Lerwick as a transhipment centre, where almost all goods entering and leaving the islands were transferred to or from the vessels which took them across the seas, was something which came relatively late, and indeed it is only since the Second World War that regular calls at other ports on the Mainland have ceased.

The history of communications within Shetland is, indeed, very closely linked with the growth of Lerwick. There had always, of course, been a certain amount of movement of men and goods from one part of the county to another, and it was carried on partly in the boats which almost every Shetlander then owned and partly by a recognised system of 'ferries' linking the islands one with another and also linking places on the Mainland which were separated from each other by voes running far into the land.[1] Neither of those systems — if the term system can properly be used of them — was based on Lerwick, for until the eighteenth century Lerwick was hardly a centre in any sense at all. By that century, however, it did have the town houses of a good many Shetland lairds, and there were merchants who had their headquarters there and conducted business throughout the islands. These individuals used their own boats to convey themselves and their property between Lerwick and other places. In 1762, for instance, the fishing station in Fetlar received its supplies of meal, biscuit and tobacco from Lerwick about once a month, by a vessel which carried fish to Lerwick on the return voyage. We also know that in the 1790s there were in Unst two decked boats, of 10-15 tons, which carried fish, salt and other commodities to and from Lerwick.

Besides, already in the early nineteenth century, Lerwick had some significance as the only post-town in the islands; it did not, indeed, as yet have a regular mail service from the south, but when any letters did reach Shetland they came to Lerwick — there to remain until they were collected. One suspects, however, that a good many letters would be carried — unofficially and illegally — by the vessels trading to and from other Shetland ports, for it has to be remembered that the smacks trading from Leith to Shetland commonly proceeded to other ports besides Lerwick. For example, the *Norna,* one of the regular Leith and Lerwick traders, usually went to the North Isles for a cargo of fish before leaving Shetland for the south, and she was lost in 1839 after she had discharged at Baltasound a part of her cargo (consisting largely of Christmas stores) and had then proceeded round the north of Unst on her way to Cullivoe. Some of the sailing vessels which traded after steam navigation was well established, such as the *Queen of the Isles,* also proceeded beyond Lerwick to the North Isles.

In the main, passengers were conveyed between Lerwick and the North Isles not by any vessels plying for hire at all, but simply in the local boats which were kept primarily for fishing and which were so plentiful, for almost everyone in the islands owned a boat or at least had a share in one. At the beginning of the nineteenth century, Dr Edmondston, at Baltasound, was the only doctor in Shetland, and when he was called on to visit patients in other islands he had to summon his neighbours to man a sixareen, a six-oared boat.[2] There were many complaints that the whole system, or lack of system, was dangerous as well as inconvenient, but there were no improvements until nearly the middle of the century. So late as 1844, a visitor who came to Shetland in the company of 'a young gentleman from that interesting country' relates that in Lerwick they 'bespoke a boat' for the purpose of conveying them further north and that it was in this sixareen that they made their way to Unst.[3] It appears that in 1839 the *Janet,* a sloop of 30 tons, began to ply from Lerwick to Unst and intermediate ports, and she was followed by better vessels of the same class, but these small sloops, or 'packets', had little accommodation or comfort for passengers. 'It was a great improvement when an old rickety sloop of some 30 to 40 tons, which had been a cod-smack, was put on the passage between Lerwick and the north isles for

a few months in summer'.[4] But even so, outside the summer
months the alternatives were still to tramp over roadless hills
and cross the ferries, to hire a sixareen, or to take one's chance
of a passage when one of the vessels plying mainly between
Shetland and the south proceeded to the North Isles.

As was the case between Lerwick and the south, mails
presented a separate problem. A post-service between Lerwick
and Unst had been established by private enterprise in 1820,
but it was a service by the overland route and the ferries, and
not by sea. In the 1840s the 'post-runner' on foot went once
a week between Unst and Lerwick, taking two days on the
journey. The same route was used for cattle and sheep, which
went on the hoof through each island in turn, crossing the
sounds by ferryboat, until they reached Lerwick, and this
practice was still followed long after the steamers had reached
Lerwick and had had an immediate effect in raising the prices
to be obtained for Shetland sheep.

It is not altogether easy to understand why the pattern of
transport beyond Lerwick developed as it did. As already
mentioned, the sailing vessels had commonly proceeded beyond
Lerwick, and when steamers were introduced, much later, on
the west side, they called at many ports besides Scalloway.
Yet on the east side there were, all through the history of
powered navigation, few exceptions to the rule that the steamer
from the south went no further than Lerwick and that the North
Isles and the east side of the north Mainland were served by a
separate vessel. The reason certainly was not the convenience
of transhipment at Lerwick, for that town had no pier at which
the steamers could berth until 1886 — long after Scalloway —
and goods had to be boated to and from the shore. Nor does the
size of the south steamers wholly explain the course of events,
because in practice most of the earlier south steamers did
deputise for the North Isles steamer from time to time, and the
west-side steamer had to work her way through many narrow
channels. At the same time, the smaller vessel was certainly
handier for a good many of the North Isles ports. Possibly one
factor was simply the time allowed for 'turn-round' at Lerwick;
it was impossible normally to handle the cargo for Lerwick and
the surrounding district and at the same time proceed round the
North Isles, though this was occasionally done.

It is suggestive of an improvement in the standard of vessels on the North Isles service that in 1864 the *Imogen*, employed on this trade, was commanded by Captain Nisbet, who soon afterwards took command of the *Matchless;* along with her were the *Lady Alice* and the *Saucy Jack*. But their practice was to leave Lerwick on Monday, potter around the islands, and return on Saturday, and there was probably no great change until the first North Isles steamers appeared with the formation of the Shetland Islands Steam Navigation Company. First came the *Chieftain's Bride*, of 94 gross tons, which made two or three trips each week to the North Isles and Yellsound ports. The attractively named *Chieftain's Bride* was known locally by the less elegant designation of 'The Crab', no doubt because she was under-powered and consequently apt to move sideways in tide-swept sounds. This pioneer went on until 1876 and, after a period when the *Lady Ambrosine* was chartered, she was suc-cccded by the first *Earl of Zetland*, built in 1877 for the Shetland Islands Steam Navigation Company, in which the North of Scotland now had a 50% holding. The vessel was taken over by the North of Scotland in 1890.

The manifold changes in the schedules of the North Isles steamer over the years would be laborious to trace in detail and tedious to recount. For most of her history, the old *Earl* made two trips weekly (usually Sunday-Monday and Friday-Saturday) to the North Isles and one to the Yellsound ports (usually Tuesday-Wednesday), though the Yellsound run was reduced to once fortnightly (Wednesday-Thursday) between the World Wars and dropped altogether thereafter. A third North Isles voyage, which had existed at times earlier, for instance in 1908, was introduced again in 1937, and after the Second War there were three North Isles trips each week. The general pattern was an outward trip one day and an inward trip the next, but there were certain exceptions: from 1892 to 1939, whereas in summer the steamer left Lerwick on Sunday afternoon and proceeded to Baltasound, returning on Monday, in winter she left Lerwick on Monday at 3 a.m. and, proceeding only to Uyea-sound, was posted to leave there at 8 a.m. and return to Lerwick the same day; the third North Isles run, in 1908, was a one-day affair on a Thursday; the Yellsound run, in its later and declining days, was also a one-day affair, on alternate Thursdays; and from 1946 the programme included a one-day round of Whalsay, Mid Yell, Brough Lodge and Uyeasound on a Wednesday, alongside the more extended two-day trips on Monday-Tuesday and Friday-Saturday.

Only two ports were called at regularly on both the North Isles and Yellsound runs — Symbister in Whalsay and Burravoe in Yell. The other places where the steamer always called on her North Isles runs were Mid Yell, Brough Lodge in Fetlar and Uyeasound in Unst; the many other ports on the North Isles runs were Gossabrough (for a time a substitute for Burravoe on some North Isles runs), Basta Voe, Gutcher, Cullivoe, Baltasound and (in early times) Haraldswick, and in the more spacious days when there was an emphasis on sight-seeing she sometimes proceeded from Haraldswick round the north and west coasts of Unst. The usual round on the Yellsound run was Burravoe, Mossbank, Ollaberry, Lochend, North Roe, Westsandwick, Ulsta, Burravoe and Vidlin, but Swinister, Sullom and Brae were each regular ports of call at various times, and calls were sometimes made at Bardister; besides, in the busy days of the herring fishing before and after 1900 the steamer sometimes continued from North Roe round to Roeness Voe and even Hillswick. There were two ports which lay off the main sailing track to the North Isles and which were fitted in in different ways at different times — Hubie in Fetlar, which was for a long time inserted between Whalsay and Burravoe on the Yellsound run, and Skerries, which at one time was fitted in fortnightly in the Yellsound run but was later a weekly port of call on one of the North Isles runs. On the North Isles runs the steamer normally lay overnight at Baltasound, sometimes at Uyeasound if that was her terminal point; on the Yellsound run she usually lay overnight at Ollaberry, sometimes at North Roe, but in earlier days at Brae.

As the traditional 'road to the isles' by steamer is now a thing of the past, after a century of existence, it is fitting that some recollections of it should be set down here. 'Leisured' is the only term suited to describe the progress of the old *Earl,* partly because she normally jogged along at about eight knots and partly because at almost every port goods, mails, passengers and cattle had to be transferred between ship and shore in 'flitboats'. For some odd reason, Shetland was overlooked when so many islands in the Orkneys and off the west coast of Scotland were equipped with piers in the nineteenth century. Even Lerwick, as already mentioned, did not have a pier until 1886, and it has been only in very recent years that public funds have been used to provide piers in the North Isles. Until after the Second World War the only point in the North Isles where the steamer could regularly come alongside was a privately-owned pier at Baltasound, though a pier at Cullivoe was used from time to time and the old *Earl* was known, on very rare occasions, to come alongside the pier at Ulsta on a flood tide. Even when the old *Earl* was replaced by the new, which was much faster on passage, the trip was still for some years mortally slow because of the time taken at ports. It is, however, right to say that there were certain exceptions to the general rule of slowness. When the *Earl* left Lerwick on Sunday at 3 p.m., as she did in summer for many years, little was handled at each call except mails and passengers, and the voyage was speeded up in consequence, though it might have a spectacular start in the great days of the herring fishing, when the steamer had to thread her way through perhaps 300 drifters anchored in Bressay Sound. It is also true that in 1937-9 she left Lerwick on Tuesday afternoons and returned on Wednesday mornings, to connect with the direct boat which then arrived in Lerwick about mid-day on Tuesday and sailed at noon on Wednesday; and on these trips there was no time for loitering. It was said, too, that the old *Earl* was actually steaming faster in her last years, and popular comment was that it no longer mattered if she burst her boiler; the present writer did, as a matter of fact, make smarter passages in her last year or two than at any earlier time.

In 1883 it was noted that it took the *Earl* from 10 a.m. to 6, 7 or 8 p.m. to make her way from Lerwick to Brae (by Whalsay, Vidlin, Burravoe, Mossbank, Ollaberry and Sullom), and between the Wars the normal pace of the service could best be studied on a Friday in summer, when the *Earl* was billed to leave Lerwick at 9 a.m. and was liable to leave at any time after about 9.30. Winding her way out of the tortuous north mouth of Bressay Sound, past Rova Head and the Brethren Rocks, she held up for the Hoo Stack and the Mull of Eswick on her way to Symbister, Whalsay, where she anchored after about an hour and twenty minutes' steaming. The Whalsay flitboat

— like most of them an old sixareen — moved slowly out, propelled by only two oars, and tied up alongside the *Earl* while goods of every description, passengers, mails and possibly cattle, were transhipped; sometimes the fltboat had to make a second trip, which meant an idle delay on the steamer while the flitboat unloaded at the pier.

At almost any port there might be a fascinating tactical struggle between the steamer's captain and the flitmen — the former trying to tempt the flitboat out, the latter trying to tempt the steamer in. The steamer gave good warning of her approach by a blast on her whistle, but the flitboat would lie at the pier as long as was decently possible, in the hope of encouraging the steamer to come farther in. Much credit was due, it should be said, to the expert seamanship of the flitmen at every port in manoeuvring their somewhat unwieldy craft alongside the steamer, often under very adverse conditions, and handling cargoes up to their maximum capacity, sometimes leaving what seemed alarmingly little freeboard. The Whalsay flitboat figured in the news after an incident on 29 December 1924, when conditions at Symbister became so severe that it was unsafe either for the *Earl* to lie there any longer or for the flitmen to take their boat back to the pier. The men were taken on board the steamer and the flitboat cut adrift — an action subsequently upheld when the owner of the flitboat sued the North of Scotland Company; but the skipper who had taken the decision went down in history as 'the man who lost the Whalsay flitboat'.

From Whalsay the direct route to the north lay by the port of Burravoe in South Yell. But for many years travellers on the Friday morning sailing, although it connected with the direct boat from Aberdeen, were humbugged by the inclusion of the Skerries in the schedule. This meant a long haul out from Whalsay, and a stretch of open North Sea which had its terrors for many passengers, though a visit to Skerries had its attractions for sightseers. It was only in 1930 that the call at Skerries was, in summer, transferred to the Monday afternoon run south (when the *Earl* had a complement of round-trippers, who might be presumed to be more interested in Skerries and less interested in reaching their destination), so that on Friday mornings the *Earl* could proceed direct from Symbister on a run of about an hour and ten minutes to Burravoe, passing *en route* the skerries off Lunna Holm from which the captain usually startled the seals by a blast on the whistle.

The Burravoe flitboat displayed a different technique from that at Whalsay, for it was more rapidly propelled by four oars. The voe here is an admirably sheltered harbour, but just too narrow and shallow at the entrance to allow the steamer to enter with ease except at high water. Consequently, there was an arrangement whereby one blast on the whistle meant that the *Earl* would come into the voe, two blasts that she would anchor outside the entrance. If the flitmen had had hopes that she would come in, the second blast always brought exclamations of disgust.

An hour's run from Burravoe, past the impressive cliffs of East Yell, brought the steamer to Mid Yell, where she would arrive between 2 and 3 p.m. (though when she went to Skerries instead of Burravoe she did not reach Mid Yell until 4 p.m. or later). At Mid Yell several flitboats plied to and from the *Earl* — one from Linkshouse, one from Gairdiesting and one from Northavoe — and they, like those at Whalsay and Burravoe, had their own technique in propulsion, for it was the habit here to rely on sails. With much business to transact, the steamer usually made a long stay in Mid Yell, and sometimes seemed to be there the better part of an afternoon.[5]

From Mid Yell it was a short run across to Brough Lodge, in Fetlar, where a short stay sufficed, as the small flitboat in use there worked from an open beach and the heavier goods for Fetlar were landed on a fortnightly call at Hubie. From Brough Lodge it was another short run to Uyeasound, at the south end of Unst, where the steamer might make quite a long stay, and from Uyeasound it was another hour's steaming to Baltasound, where passengers who were wearied by a journey from Lerwick which had taken most of the day were at least able to step ashore, in the evening, on a pier, instead of waiting until a flitboat was first loaded with goods.

On Saturday morning the steamer left Baltasound at 6 o'clock, and worked her way south, usually by Uyeasound, Cullivoe, Brough Lodge, Mid Yell, Burravoe and Whalsay, to Lerwick. As there was much less cargo to handle on the southward trip, better time was made, and the ship might arrive at Lerwick in the early afternoon — except, however, in the lamb-shipping season, or, in earlier years, in the herring season, when she might be badly detained through making special calls to collect cured herring at the various stations which then operated.

Indeed, if 'leisured' is one appropriate adjective to describe the North Isles service, 'unpredictable' is another. The vessel was not only at the mercy of the trade, but at the beck of even a single passenger, who was often obliged by a special call (even if it involved fitting in Hubie between Skerries and Mid Yell, or Burravoe between Mid Yell and Skerries). When one stepped on board the *Earl* one was never quite certain where one was going to go and when one's voyage would end. For passengers waiting at an intermediate port for the steamer to take them to Lerwick, the hour at which she would turn up was also unpredictable. At Burravoe, for instance, one knew that she was liable to appear as early as 10.30 a.m. (indeed it was said that on one legendary occasion she had been in Burravoe at 10.10 a.m.), and one had to be there in readiness from that time onwards. Before the days of telephones (which reached the North Isles only in the later 1930s), an obliging postmistress was very helpful, with the telegraph. 'Tinkle, tinkle', went the machine, and one was informed that 'she left Uyeasound at 8 o'clock', or 'she was in Cullivoe at 10 o'clock', or received the depressing message, 'she's not come to Cullivoe yet' or the satisfactory news that 'she left Mid Yell a little ago'. But one might spend the greater part of the day waiting for the steamer, and one might even wait in vain, if, after all, she went past one's port in the end either because of fog or because of heavy weather.

There was a remarkably friendly and intimate atmosphere about the old *Earl*. The strong community feeling among Shetlanders is noticeable enough even on the 'south boat', but it was much stronger on the North Isles steamer, where most of the passengers were drawn from an even more restricted community. There was, too, an unusual degree of fellowship between the passengers and the ship's company, not least the captain, who was well acquainted with the regular travellers. The ship, as it happened, had hand-steering, and two men had sometimes to be put on the wheel in heavy weather (though, even so, a kick from the wheel could dislocate the bo'sun's shoulder on a dirty morning). Although there was a flying bridge on top of the captain's cabin, with the engine-room telegraph on it (so that the captain had to take command from there on entering and leaving ports), the steering wheel was on deck, in front of the captain's cabin, and there was no wheelhouse until the Second World War. The captain therefore normally stood among the passengers while he gave his orders. This produced a sense of being 'all in it together' and removed any mystery from navigation. Much greater mystery always seemed to attach to the management of the cargo, for it was a puzzle how such an infinite variety of goods, large and small, could be recorded and find their way to their appointed destination at any one of half-a-dozen or more ports. All one could see was that different areas in the 'tween-decks were allocated to goods for the various ports, to facilitate the correct allocation of cargo. Much the same arrangement prevailed on MacBrayne's Sound of Mull steamer, which used to trade from Oban to Craignure, Lochaline, Salen, Drimmin and Tobermory. One day, so it is said, a man came on board with a packet for Salen and laid it down at a certain point, to be rebuked by a member of the crew with the words, 'No, don't put it there. That part of the ship is not going to Salen'. That in turn brings to mind a witty retort by Captain Andrew Ramsay when in command of the twin-screw *St Ninian*. A passenger in the wheelhouse remarked that the two rev. counters showed different readings, and was informed 'that side of the ship will get to Leith first'.

Among the successive captains of the old *Earl* (many of whom served subsequently as masters of 'south boats'), perhaps the best remembered is William Spence, who did more than one spell as her master in the period after the First World War and finished his career in her in the late twenties and early thirties of this century after having been in command of the *St Ninian* (I) and *St Sunniva* (I). As befitted a man who had served in sailing vessels in many parts of the world and had had gruelling experiences which a man of poorer character and physique would not have survived, Spence was an intrepid skipper, who disliked nothing so much as to be held up by bad weather, and he could find his way, in all conditions, through tortuous, rock-strewn channels. It was surely Spence who was skipper on the occasion when the anemometer in Lerwick registered a wind speed of 102 miles an hour and then choked with snow but the *Earl's* log read 'Stiff breeze from nor-east'.

Spence's principal diversion was pulling the legs of the tourists, in reply to their many questions. One Monday afternoon, as the vessel entered Skerries, a tourist, pointing to the shore-station for the lighthouse, asked 'What is that building?' and was solemnly informed, 'Oh, that — that's a hotel'. And an hour or so later, approaching Whalsay, a tourist drew the captain's attention to rigs overgrown with yellow weed and asked, 'What crop is that?', to be told 'That's mustard. They sell it to Colman's. That's just a sideline'. On another occasion, in conversation with a man who asked what kind of people lived in Skerries, Spence said, 'Oh, terrible people. You know, we never lie here overnight.' 'Why not?' 'They'd come aboard and scalp us'. One day off Fetlar, when a member of the flitboat's crew was a particularly hirsute individual, Spence solemnly informed a German visitor, who was conscientiously taking notes, 'That's one of the industries here, growing human hair. They sell it for a shilling a pound'. For Spence to tell the truth was sometimes a visible strain. One rather misty Sunday afternoon, on the passage between Symbister and Burravoe, a tourist discerned the faint shape of land to starboard, looking incredibly remote, and asked the captain 'What land is that?'. There was a perceptible hesitation while Spence may have toyed with the idea of saying it was the Norwegian coast before he answered truthfully, 'That's Skerries'.

Some particulars of the old *Earl* will be found in Part II of this book, but cold figures can hardly do justice to the place she held in the life, and indeed the affection, of the North Isles people for so long. A vessel could hardly have survived nearly seventy years of service in those waters, in the days when there was neither echometer nor radar and almost everything depended on the skilled judgment of the master, without occasional strandings, but the *Earl* recovered triumphantly from the few accidents she did have. Some of her mishaps were commemorated in verse:

'She gaed on Robbie Ramsay's Baa,
In Baltasoond she brak in twa:
They put a bit into her middle
And made her fit as ony fiddle'.[6]

The lengthening of the ship took place in 1884, though

apparently not in consequence of a mishap in Baltasound; and the stranding on Robbie Ramsay's Baa (a rock in the north mouth of Lerwick harbour) occurred in 1924. The incident best remembered by some is her stranding on Lunna Holm one foggy day in 1912. When the vessel came to rest on the grassy islet, a local worthy who was on board turned to the mate and asked, 'Boy, is du tinkin tae gie her a corn o' green girse i' da morning?'[7] The one recorded incident at Baltasound was a peculiar one, on 8 June 1902, when the herring fishing was in full swing. In the crowded harbour the *Earl* struck an old ballast heap, and, though the damage seemed negligible, she filled with alarming speed and had to be towed to Aberdeen for repair.

The old *Earl* had been hailed on her advent as 'a powerful and commodious steamer',[8] and no doubt she seemed to be so to those whose memories went back to the smacks; but long before her career in the North Isles ended she was not unreasonably criticised as hopelessly outdated. The only permanent sleeping accommodation was a small Ladies' Cabin; gentlemen had to make do with berths in the Saloon, except in the touring season, when a temporary Gentlemen's Cabin was rigged up in the 'tween-decks beside the after hatch. On deck there was no shelter for passengers — or, for that matter, for the officer on watch. It all had its appeal to those who believed that sea travel involved plenty of fresh air, but a generation arose which had different standards. The predominantly slow and erratic character of the steamer's movements also led to growing impatience on the part of the twentieth-century travelling public. Yet attempts to compete with her and offer alternatives were long unsuccessful. In the early years of this century, the *Norseman,* which competed with the south steamers, also ran in the North Isles, but her career was short, and the experiment of the Shetland sheep-rearing interest in 1932 in chartering the *Great Western,* which made some calls in the North Isles as well as at Lerwick, was not repeated. In the early 1930s a motor vessel, the *Majestic,* later re-named *Innovator,* competed for two or three years in goods traffic, but with no enduring success. Peculiarly ill-fated was the motor boat *Islander,* introduced in 1931 and, carrying passengers only, seeming to offer the opportunity of smarter passages. One Sunday afternoon she broke down off the Brethren, outside the north mouth of Bressay Sound, and had to be ignominiously taken in tow by the *Earl;* and she finally came to grief one Saturday morning when she ran hard and fast on a rock off Aywick.

The most serious rival in the end was the 'overland route' by road and ferry. That route, which had been utilised for the earliest North Isles mail service, had never been wholly superseded by the steamer, for some at least of the North Isles mails went 'overland' until 1937 and the route was always used occasionally by travellers who either dreaded the sea or could not wait a day or two for the steamer. The service for the mails on Wednesday was patronised by a lot of people, for the steamer at that time offered no connection with the direct boat arriving in Lerwick on Tuesday — except that once a fortnight the *Earl* left Lerwick on Wednesday for Whalsay, Hubie, Burravoe and Yellsound. As long as the sounds were crossed by open sailing boats and the roads were execrably bad, there was little chance that this route would draw much traffic from the *Earl,* but already in the 1930s, with motor ferry boats and gradually improving roads, at least between Lerwick and Mossbank, an appreciable number of passengers chose the overland route, even although, except on Wednesday, it usually meant the expense of private hire of car and boat. It was the growing challenge of this service which caused the Shipping Company to institute the *Earl's* Tuesday-Wednesday sailing to connect with the direct boat. It was said that this piece of enterprise was the idea of David Gray, the *Earl's* purser, who was so importunate that in the end he was told he could take the *Earl* to Uyeasound or anywhere else on a Tuesday afternoon.

Saturday, 19 August 1939, was a day which will never be forgotten by those who were present in Lerwick then, for a new *Earl* was at last to replace the old one and she was to be welcomed with considerable ceremonial. The old *Earl,* under the command of Captain Spence, who had been recalled from his retirement for the occasion, had come down from the North Isles in the early afternoon, and later left the Victoria pier with the *St Sunniva* (Captain William Gifford) to rendezvous off Mousa with the *St Magnus* (Captain D. McMillan) and the new *Earl of Zetland* (commanded by Captain Thomas Gifford, who had succeeded Spence on the old *Earl*). The four ships, each dressed overall, formed in line ahead and proceeded into Lerwick harbour, led by the little old *Earl,* followed by the new *Earl,* the *St Magnus* and the *St Sunniva.*

The old *Earl* made what was intended to be her last trip on Sunday-Monday, and when she left Lerwick on the Monday evening Shetland thought it had said goodbye to the old ship. But a fortnight later the Second World War began. Early in 1940 the new *Earl* was requisitioned for service on the Pentland Firth, and the old *Earl* was recalled, to serve for another six years and more, to the beginning of 1946.

It was thought that with the arrival of the new *Earl* a new and better era in North Isles travel had opened. But the fact was that the new ship had come too late. Already there had been a tendency for passenger traffic to prefer the speedier journey by bus and ferry, though it was far less comfortable than a passage in the new *Earl,* and war conditions accelerated the drift away from the old sea-route. After the Second World War, conditions became still less favourable to the traditional 'road to the Isles'. The 'overland service' by bus and ferry came to be much better organised, with larger buses, larger boats on Yellsound and Bluemull Sound, tarmacadam roads, and safer piers for the ferry crossings — all at considerable expense in rates and taxes. On the steamer route, by contrast, the aged sixareens which had served so long as flitboats were wearing out and the cost of replacement was almost prohibitive, while the wages and national insurance contributions of the flitmen also became an item which the merchants at the smaller ports could not face; the number of ports of call was therefore reduced, and motor flitboats were gradually introduced at those which remained. Action to compensate for the loss of the minor ports by providing adequate piers for the steamer at the more important ports was too late and too ineffective; for example, a pier was not completed at Mid Yell until some three years after calls at Burravoe ceased (in 1950), and it then proved unsuitable for use at all states of the tide; and a pier at Symbister was not completed until 1966.

The Shipping Company seems to have decided that it was not worth while trying to compete with the growing popularity of the 'overland service', and devised a schedule after the Second War which was not designed to suit the convenience of passengers, as it provided no connection with the direct boat arriv-

ing in Lerwick on Tuesday morning and none with either of
the indirect boats. Consequently, ordinary travellers, making a
journey on business or on holiday, ceased to be found in great
numbers on the North Isles steamer, though in summer she was
still well filled with tourists doing a round trip. The atmosphere
remained singularly friendly, business was conducted without
fuss or formality, and the voyage retained its attraction for the
visitor, to whom it gave an unrivalled view of the scenery and
an insight into the islands' life. Once it was evident that the
Earl's days were numbered and that her withdrawal would be
a great loss to tourism, there were devotees who never missed
an opportunity to make yet another trip.

The first *Earl* had been relieved in earlier days by one or
other of the south boats, and from 1928 by the *St Clement* (I);
during the Second War she was twice relieved by the *Earl
Sigurd* (1942, 1943). The second *Earl* was relieved by the *St
Rognvald* (III) on one occasion, but chiefly by the *St Clement*
(II) and later by the *St Ola* (II). That sea transport within
Shetland was still of value in an emergency was demonstrated
during two winters after the Second War. In 1947, when nearly
all the roads in the county were completely blocked by heavy
snow, recourse was perforce had to the old means of communication, and the *Earl of Zetland* (II), besides calling at all
ports in the North Isles, made a round of the Mainland to
deliver essential supplies at each centre of population. When
similar circumstances arose in a later winter, one of the Fishery
Protection Vessels was pressed into use for the same purpose.

As the vehicle-ferries linking the North Isles were introduced one by one, the *Earl* was withdrawn stage by stage — from
Yell in August 1973, from Unst in December 1973, from Fetlar
and Skerries about a year later, and she finally ran only to
Symbister. Because she thus went out with a whimper rather
than a bang, there was no question of the kind of spectacular
farewell to correspond with the greetings which had accompanied
her arrival in 1939 (though the town band was out when she
left her familiar berth at Victoria Pier for the last time on 3
March 1975). Yet her passing was viewed with much genuine
regret. I happened to be in Mid Yell when she made her last
scheduled call there in August 1973. As I walked down the pier
to meet her, I overtook two local women who were recalling
in their conversation, as I was recalling in my mind, the high

15. *St Magnus (II)*

16   *St Margaret (I)*

17. *St Margaret (II)*

18 St Magnus (III)

hopes with which the ship had been welcomed when she arrived in 1939. One said to the other, 'Weel, we'll maybe be waar aff'. Perhaps the perfect epitaph for the ninety-eight years of service given to the North Isles by two successive *Earls*.

REFERENCES

1 Donaldson, *Shetland under Earl Patrick*, 46; O'Dell, *Historical Geography of Shetland*, 317.
2 Edmondston gives the hire charges.
3 Manson's *Shetland Almanac for 1934*, 221-2.
4 Biot Edmondston and Jessie M. E. Saxby, *Home of a Naturalist*, 123.
5 A photograph of the *Earl* lying in Mid Yell was reproduced in the first edition of this book and also in my *Shetland Life under Earl Patrick*.
6 The complete verses were printed in *The Shetland News* in August 1939. The lines I have quoted represent a slightly different version, as I recall hearing them from an old lady in South Yell some years earlier.
7 The phrase is one that might be used of feeding a cow; 'Are you thinking to give her a drop of green grass in the morning?'.
8 *Home of a Naturalist*, 135.

F

Chapter Seven

CRUISES AND EXCURSIONS

While tourists had been making use of the regular steamer services to the islands from their earliest days, little if anything seems to have been done to arrange sailings specifically for the tourist until the regular services had reached considerable proportions, as they did by 1883. Then, as part of the phase of energetic expansion which followed within a few years, the Company entered on a programme which lacked nothing in ambition, for its first efforts broke completely new ground by arranging cruises to Norway.

The *St Rognvald* (I) was advertised in 1886 to leave Leith on 20 June for a ten-day cruise to the Hardanger, Sogne and Romsdal Fjords, at an inclusive cost of £10. This was a pioneering venture in the fullest sense, for it appears that this was actually the first Norwegian cruise organised by any British shipping line. Four other trips were made during the first season, the last of them beginning on 1 August. The *St Rognvald*, built in 1883, was not ill-fitted for the programme on which she now entered. She was far the largest ship yet built for the Company — and, indeed, was not substantially exceeded in tonnage until the appearance of the *St Magnus* (III) in 1924. After the Norwegian cruises started she underwent considerable alterations, and the ultimate result was to provide first-class accommodation extending from the stern to the forward hatch, including a dining saloon with seating for some eighty persons, and 108 berths, mainly in two-berth cabins. There were also three baths, reckoned an unusual feature in those days, and an organ in the saloon as well as a piano in the 'Music Room'.

The experiment of 1886 was so successful that the Company at once ordered the building of the first *St Sunniva* as a purely passenger vessel, and she came into service in the following year, providing a series of ten-day Norwegian cruises all through the summer from June to September; her 'sixth ten-day trip' left on 28 July. The new ship, with no cargo space at all

and with passenger accommodation on the lower deck as well
as the main deck, had a saloon seating nearly 130 persons — that
is, approximately the number which could sleep in her 132 beds
(arranged in two-berth and four-berth cabins and a Ladies'
Cabin with ten berths). Like the *St Rognvald*, she had three
baths, but although there was a piano there was no organ. It
was perhaps more to the point that she carried a steam launch
for boating at places where she could not berth alongside a
wharf.

For more than ten years the *St Rognvald* as well as the *St
Sunniva* was used for cruising, though the latter vessel, which
was used exclusively on cruises, carried the greater part of the
work. The programme, while mainly of Norwegian cruises, was
developed in various ways. In 1891, for example, the *St Sunniva*
was scheduled for a long cruise to the Baltic (29 August to 23
September), at a fare of £35, with 'one cabin for each passenger'.
In 1894 there were seven Norwegian cruises, all but one by
the *St Sunniva,* starting on dates from 7 June to 18 August,
from Leith but calling at Aberdeen on the return voyage and
on two occasions calling at Lerwick on the return voyage. The
itinerary always included Stavanger, Odde, Hardanger Fjord,
Bergen, Gudvangen, Romsdal and Molde, but sometimes
included Eide, Fjaerland Fjord, Geiranger Fjord and Trondheim.
In 1898 the *St Sunniva* was scheduled for seven Norwegian
cruises, on dates from 17 May to 8 August. She started from
Leith, and it is significant of her speed that she was scheduled
to sail from Aberdeen only six hours after her departure from
Leith; at Aberdeen she either went alongside or anchored off
while passengers were brought out, according to the tide. The
itinerary included usually Odde, Bergen, Gudvangen, Oie and
Geiranger, Romsdal and Molde, and sometimes Stavanger, Sand,
Balholmen or Fjaerland, Visnaes, Nordfjord and Trondheim.
The *St Rognvald* was billed for a more ambitious cruise to the
North Cape, from Leith on 21 June, by way of Odde, Bergen,
Gudvangen, Romsdal and Molde, Trondheim, Tromso, Ham-
merfest, Lofoten, Christiansund, Geiranger and Oie, returning
on 8 July. Besides, there were two cruises, one by the *St
Rognvald* from 25 May to 18 June and the other by the *St
Sunniva* from 20 August to 13 September, to the Baltic and
Northern Capitals — Oslo, Copenhagen, Stockholm and St.
Petersburg. In 1903 there were six cruises, all by the *St Sunniva,*

on dates from 3 June to 4 August, departing from Leith and (except the first cruise) from Aberdeen, to Odde, Bergen (on both outward and homeward voyage), Gudvangen, Geiranger, Molde and sometimes Sand, Visnaes and Trondheim. The fare for a ten-day Fjord cruise ranged from £15 for a single cabin down to £10 10s. for each person in cabins for more than two persons; for the cruises to the North Cape and the Baltic the rates were double or more. The passage money included morning tea or coffee, breakfast, lunch, tea, dinner and late tea or coffee, and passengers were assured that 'the cuisine is equal to that of a first-class hotel'. A deposit of £3 was required on booking and the balance was payable six days before departure. Several shore excursions were available in Norway at additional charges. Besides people doing the round cruise, passengers were carried between Scottish ports and ports in Norway and the changes in the itinerary rather suggest that this side of the business may have become more important as the years passed.

The advertisements pointed out that 'these vessels take all the inside passages, thereby keeping in smooth water, and reach the head of the fiords, which larger vessels are precluded from doing'. However, vessels of such limited capacity were driven out of the business by the competition of larger ships, and the *St Sunniva* ended her Norwegian cruises in 1908. This phase in the Company's history was long remembered — and indeed geography almost dictated that it should be thought of as an obvious activity for the 'North' Company. It was proposed to send the *St Ninian* (II) on two trips to Norway in May 1951, but insufficient support was forthcoming.

During the period when the cruises operated, it was almost customary, after the season for northern cruises was over, to arrange a cruise round Great Britain. This was done for the first time, it seems, in August-September 1901, and probably in each year following — certainly in 1901, 1903, 1905, 1906, 1907 and 1908; in the last of those years there were two cruises round Britain. The itinerary of the 1903 cruise was from Leith to Tilbury, Torquay, Dartmouth, Isle of Man, Greenock, Rothesay, Oban, Skye, Stromness, Aberdeen, Leith and back to Tilbury; it lasted from 15 August to 1 September and the fares ranged down from £20. The 1907 cruise went from Leith to Gravesend, Torquay, Falmouth, Dublin, Isle of Man, Greenock, Oban, Stornoway, Stromness, Aberdeen, Leith and Gravesend.

Besides such autumn cruises, the *St Sunniva* did Mediterranean cruises, evidently on charter, in at least two winters.

Rather oddly, special cruises within the islands where the Company transacted most of its business emerged later than the more ambitious ventures further afield (though excursions between Orkney and Caithness, not organised by the 'North' Company, appeared as early as 1860-2). In 1894 the *St Nicholas* was advertised for cruises of less than a week's duration, including Fair Isle and Foula, leaving Leith on 20 and 27 August. In 1895 and 1896 the *St Rognvald* made a cruise of this type, from Leith to Aberdeen, Fair Isle, Scalloway, Foula, Hillswick, Lerwick and Kirkwall; it was stated that no cargo was carried, and the fare for the round was £5. The *St Sunniva* was billed for a cruise round Shetland at the end of August 1897, and again in 1898.

Quite a distinct development, apart from the provision of special cruises and excursions, was the offer of travel on the Company's normal services at reduced rates. These appeared as early as 1862, when they were offered from Kirkwall to Granton, and they were associated particularly with the passage between Aberdeen and Leith. At least as early as July 1885 we find that excursion fares were offered from Leith to Aberdeen in connection with the Royal Highland Show. At what stage such fares came to be regularly offered at the times of the Aberdeen and Edinburgh Trades Holidays does not appear, but they were a constant feature of the Company's programme for many years and continued until 1955. The popularity of the steamer trip between Leith and Aberdeen was such that in many years additional sailings were put on from Leith at the time of the Trades Holidays; several were advertised in 1902; for example. Extra sailings were especially useful between the Wars, when there was no regular steamer from Leith on a Saturday, though the direct boat then offered a day-time voyage from Leith to Aberdeen on Monday and one from Aberdeen to Leith on Sunday. In recent years excursion fares have been offered from time to time for a return from Lerwick to Aberdeen on the occasion of a holiday in Lerwick.

In 1886, the same year which saw the first Norwegian cruises, the Company was advertising a range of 'Special Tourist Tickets', some of which set the pattern for the 'round trips' which have been almost constant ever since. From Leith to

Lerwick or Scalloway and back cost £3 3s. inclusive of provisions, from Leith to Hillswick or the North Isles and back
cost £3 15s. The ordinary return fares from Leith to Lerwick
or Scalloway at that time were £1 19s. and from Aberdeen
£1 11s. 6d., first class; the second class returns were 15s. 9d.
and 12s. 9d. There was also in 1886 a kind of maritime equivalent
of the 'Freedom of Scotland' tickets sometimes issued by British
Rail: for the sum of £4 10s. one could travel for a fortnight
on any of the Company's services.

In 1898 an elaborate series of round trips was advertised,
making use of all the Company's routes to and from Shetland
and between Lerwick and the North Isles, in various combina-
tions: for example, one could switch from the *Earl of Zetland*
at Ollaberry to the west side steamer at Hillswick, or one could
spend four successive days (Sunday to Wednesday) on the *Earl,*
doing first the round of the North Isles and then the round of
Yellsound.

A new era opened with the erection of the Company's Hotel
at Hillswick, which was first advertised in 1902. This led at
once to the institution of inclusive holidays, combining the trip
on the west-side steamer with a week at Hillswick. It is probably
significant that, after three years during which the *St Nicholas*
operated on this route, the duty was transferred to the newer
St Ninian, which carried it on down to 1914. After the First
World War the *St Rognvald* was the west-side and Hillswick
steamer in summer from 1925 until 1936 (except in 1930), and
then the new *St Clair* (II) was put on — the first time a new ship
had been assigned to this route. In 1908, when the cost of a
five-day cruise by either the *St Ninian* (on the west side) or
the *St Rognvald* (on the east side) was £3 10s., and the weekly
terms at the hotel were £3 3s., the charge for an eleven day
holiday, with a week at Hillswick, was £6 6s. Between the wars,
inclusive fares were available on all the main-line ships, including
the Caithness one. The charge for a round trip from Leith to
Shetland was then £7 10s., and for a cruise and a week at
Hillswick it was £12 10s.

After the Second War it was this side of the holiday business
that the Company greatly developed. For a short time it owned,
besides Hillswick, the Standing Stones Hotel in Orkney, but use
was made in the main of a variety of hotels in Shetland under
independent ownership — at Sumburgh, Scalloway, Sullom,

Mid Yell, Baltasound and Uyeasound (none of them continuously). A great range of holidays was on offer, combining various sailings of the Kirkwall boats and the direct boat with round trips on the *Earl of Zetland* and with residence at one or another hotel. The cessation of the passenger service from Leith *via* Orkney led to a great reduction in this kind of business, but it was soon revived, as the next chapter will show.

While inclusive holidays, and cruises on the regular services, developed, the special cruise all but disappeared. Between the Wars, it was almost unknown for any of the main-line ships to make any trips except on her normal mail-and-cargo services. Once or twice the *St Magnus* (III), which was the weekend boat and normally lay in Lerwick from Saturday to Monday, made an excursion to Uyeasound and round Unst on the Sunday. The *St Clair* (I), when on the Caithness run, occasionally made a trip on a Wick holiday to a port on the south side of the Moray Firth, and the vessel on the west side run in early summer was sometimes advertised for an excursion from Scalloway to Foula. Nor was much done within Shetland, though the old *Earl of Zetland* made an occasional cruise round Bressay and Noss, and her time-table was adjusted on the day of the Fetlar show each year to enable people from Lerwick, Whalsay or Yell to spend a day in Fetlar.

After the Second War, several experiments were made in the way of cruises by the *Earl of Zetland* (II) in Shetland waters. The plan, for two or three summers, was for three long excursions from Lerwick on Sundays — to Fair Isle, Foula and round Unst; but the weather was the unpredictable factor, and it was only in one season that all three excursions proved successful. A cruise to Baltasound and round the Flugga was planned at the time of the Historical Congress in 1969, but it also had to be cancelled because of the weather. The Shetland Antiquarian Society was more fortunate, and made special cruises to Fair Isle and Fetlar. The *Earl's* one-day round of the islands on Wednesday provided the equivalent of a cruise from Lerwick, and by a slight adjustment of the time-table it was possible to provide excursions from time to time from the North Isles to Lerwick and back on a Tuesday; the latter arrangement also enabled anyone from Yell, Unst or Fetlar to have a day in Whalsay. On one occasion the time-table was adjusted to provide time ashore at Skerries (after calls at Whalsay, Mid Yell and

Uyeasound). A special cruise on Thursday evenings in summer round Bressay and Noss was a regular feature for several years after the War.

The *St Ola* (II) operated various excursions, though rarely in her later years. The *Orcadia* (III) has also been used for cruising occasionally, to Fair Isle among other places, and on the occasion of the Historical Congress in Kirkwall in 1968 she made a special trip to Rousay, Egilsay and Wyre.

Chapter Eight

THE SHAPING OF A NEW PATTERN, 1967-1977

'The writing is on the wall for the North of Scotland too'. The speaker was a Shetlander who had all his life been closely associated with the North of Scotland ships. His father had served on the first *Earl of Zetland,* he himself had served on the *St Sunniva* (I) in her cruising days and his brother had been her master during part of her later career. The date of his remark was 1955 and the occasion was the news that, contrary to earlier reports, the *St Rognvald* (III) was to have accommodation for only twelve passengers. He saw that fact, correctly enough, in the context of the general decline of passenger services all round the British coast after the Second World War.

The events of the next thirty years seemed in many ways to fulfil the prediction, for it was easy enough to see stage by stage the reduction of the traditional passenger trade. The second *St Rognvald* had been a passenger and cargo vessel of the old type, but the third (as just mentioned) was a cargo vessel carrying only twelve passengers; the fourth *St Magnus* (formerly the second *St Clair* and in her day the Company's finest passenger steamship) was replaced by a purely cargo vessel, the fifth *St Magnus;* the second *St Ninian,* a commodious passenger ship, was not replaced at all. Even the twelve-passenger *St Clement* (II) was disposed of, and the sale of the *Earl of Zetland* (II) meant the loss of yet another passenger ship. Consequently, by 1977 passenger services were provided by only two ships, the third *St Ola* and the fourth *St Clair* — though the *St Rognvald* (then over twenty years old) still had her twelve passengers. It was a big change from 1913, when the Company had nine passenger ships, or even from 1939, when it had six (plus one twelve-passenger ship).

It is true, too, that the reduction of the passenger fleet had the effect of completely effacing the pattern of services which had developed during the expansion of steam navigation and which had still survived, though with some important modification, after 1945. In 1956, the year after the third *St*

Rognvald appeared, there had been the withdrawal of services
from Leith and Aberdeen to Caithness, after nearly a hundred
and thirty years. This, however, was of limited significance, and
the first major blow was the disposal of the *St Magnus* (IV) in
1967 and her replacement by a cargo vessel. This meant the end,
also after a hundred and thirty years, of the 'weekend boat'
which had so long — though latterly only in summer — brought
passengers from the south to Lerwick on a Saturday. 'No boat
coming in to Lerwick on a Saturday night!' some exclaimed.
It seemed hardly conceivable.

What was perhaps even more poignant — if that is the word
— about the disposal of the fourth *St Magnus* was that it was the
end of steam, which had so long seemed inseparable from sea
travel that the word 'steamer' has been retained, seemingly with
universal agreement, to designate vessels where there is no
steam except in the galleys. The sweet-running triple-expansion
engine had been almost noiseless and so free from vibration
that one sometimes wondered momentarily 'Has she stopped?'
Some had taken badly at first to the incessant throb of the
diesel. On the other hand, in contrast to the silent modern
electric cranes, the old steam cranes created a clattering din
which could be heard over half the town when a vessel was
working cargo at Kirkwall or Lerwick on a quiet day. One of
my treasured possessions is a tape recording of all the characteristic noises I heard on the last occasion I sailed from Aberdeen
on the Company's last steamship: the persistent clatter of the
cranes, the three successive bells, the factory whistles of Aberdeen (for the hour was twelve noon), the repeated clang of
the engine-room telegraph, a barely perceptible sound as the
main engine started, and then the cries of the gulls as we moved
down the channel. I believe that the late Mr Ernest Marwick
made a similar recording.

However, although steam had gone, the *St Ninian* (II)
continued, summer and winter, on what had since the Second
World War become the chief service from Leith to Aberdeen,
Kirkwall and Lerwick, and it was hoped and expected that this
at least would go on and long continue to give pleasure to 'round-
trippers' week by week, as well as providing a refuge, especially
from Kirkwall on a Friday evening, for fog-bound and frustrated
would-be travellers by air — and turning up in Leith with
train-like regularity at 4.15 on Saturday afternoon. It was with

a sense of shock — with, as Lord Birsay wrote, 'a deep sense of frustration and anger' — that we learned in 1970 that the *St Ninian* was to go and that all services from Leith, cargo as well as passenger, would end in the following spring. The *St Ninian* actually finished her work for the North of Scotland Company with a spell deputising for the *St Clair* (III) on the direct run, and it was the *St Rognvald* that was the last ship to convey passengers from Aberdeen to Leith, on 27 February 1971.

Meantime there were changes in the management of the ships. The North of Scotland Company was taken over by Coast Lines in 1961 and ten years later Coast Lines was absorbed by P. & O. Some Shetlanders felt that there was a certain appropriateness about the latter merger, since Arthur Anderson, a Shetlander with very humble origins, had been one of the founders of the P. & O. Company and had been a benefactor of Lerwick with the Anderson Educational Institute and the Widows' Homes, both of them on sites overlooking the ships as they pass into and out of Lerwick. When, on 1 October 1975, the North of Scotland, Orkney and Shetland Shipping Company finally became known as 'P. & O. Ferries, Orkney and Shetland Services', the Company issued an advertisement recalling Arthur Anderson and assuring passengers that 'the change of name is the only change you'll notice'. In truth, it was only stage by stage that changes were noticed. The merger with Coast Lines in 1961 caused no change at all, at any rate none visible to passengers on the ships. Even when P. & O. took over there was for a time little perceptible difference. The first change noticeable by passengers was, oddly enough, on the dining tables, where china with the kind of maze pattern already familiar to those who had cruised on P. & O. ships, was introduced in place of the old cups and saucers with the 'North' Company's name on them; the colours, however, were still the familiar blue and white. The P. & O. flag next appeared at the jackstaff, while the old North of Scotland flag retained its place at the mast-head — a decent compromise. But the revolution came with the change to 'P. & O. Ferries' in 1975, when most of the remaining vestiges of the old Company soon vanished. Blue funnels displaced the yellow which had been familiar for a generation and more, and the blue and white flags were now superseded at the mastheads as well. Officers' caps, however, still retained the

North of Scotland badge, and the old flag could still be seen, alongside the P. & O. flag, at Aberdeen. There was overwhelming relief that the reported threat to abandon 'Saint' names in favour of animal-names was not carried out.

But the 'new look' was not merely superficial. The fact is that the story of the last decade, while it seems at first sight a story of retreat, was rather one of the re-shaping of the services to take account of modern needs. The introduction of vehicle-carrying vessels, in place of conventional passenger and cargo ships, was overdue, and indeed some thought that with more foresight the Company might have made provision on the *St Clair* (III) to meet a demand which has in the end proved to be the salvation of the passenger trade. The *St Clair* was regularly carrying 30 to 40 cars, but they had all to be laboriously lifted and lowered by crane and the number she could take became quite inadequate in the summer season. As the 'sixties wore on, and as drive-through vessels were steadily taking over on routes elsewhere, there was growing talk of replacing the existing North of Scotland vessels by vehicle-carriers of one kind or another. Fulfilment was long deferred, partly because of the high costs of such ships and partly because of the need to construct appropriate ramps and other facilities at the terminal ports.

Plans for the Pentland Firth crossing took effect first, and the third *St Ola* appeared in January 1975. Specially designed for the work, she has accommodation for 400 passengers and can carry over 90 cars.[1] For the Aberdeen-Lerwick service a new ship was ordered but did not materialise. The problem was growing ever more acute with the transformation of the Shetland economy owing to oil developments, and among other solutions proposed was the adaptation of the *Lion,* which was to be withdrawn from the Ardrossan-Belfast run; but the *Lion* did not have sleeping accommodation on the necessary scale and would therefore have required extensive reconstruction. Ultimately the *Panther,* formerly on the Southampton-San Sebastian service, became the fourth *St Clair* in 1977. Fully half as big again in tonnage as her predecessor, and 100 feet longer, this ship has accommodation for 700 passengers and a vehicle capacity of 200 cars or 30 heavy lorries. In her first season the maximum number of passengers she actually carried on any one trip was 625; as to vehicles, she was usually 90% full on passages north and 70% full on return voyages. While her initial schedule was identical with that which had persisted from 1946 — leaving Aberdeen on Monday and Thursday and Lerwick on Tuesday and Saturday (but at 6 p.m., not the traditional 5) — hopes were held out from the outset that she would do three trips a week if the traffic required it. Already in her first season she several times made an extra run (which, with her reserve of power and her quick 'turn-round', she could easily fit in), and at the end of 1977 took up a regular thrice-weekly schedule — Monday, Wednesday and Friday from Aberdeen and Tuesday, Thursday and Saturday from Lerwick. The *St Clair* and the *St Ola* together have a tonnage almost equal to that of the entire fleet of nine vessels of 1914. The *St Clair's* captain remarked that her bow-thrust unit has a horse-power nearly as great as that of the main engine of the *Earl of Zetland* (II).

The terminal jetties for the drive-through ships meant little change from the site of the old berths at Scrabster and Stromness, but at Lerwick and Aberdeen there was a revolution. At Aberdeen, the limited space available at Matthews' Quay had long put almost intolerable pressure on operations, and the new facilities were constructed at Jamieson's Quay, very near the top of the harbour and incomparably more convenient for the Railway Station as well as adjacent to the approach road from the south. At Lerwick, the change was to a site at Holmsgarth, at the north end of the town, which was almost correspondingly inconvenient (except indeed to those who, on driving off, want to head immediately for the north Mainland or the North Isles). The facilities at Holmsgarth, including waiting-rooms and cafeteria for passengers, are excellent, but Lerwegians feel that they have lost something now that the south boat no longer lies in almost the centre of the waterfront, constantly visible and almost dominating the scene.

The four vessels which have successively borne the name *St Clair* among them epitomise the developments of coastal passenger vessels over a century and more. Each represented an innovation, at least so far as the 'North' boats were concerned, and each was typical of her period. The *St Clair* of 1868 was the first of the Company's screw vessels to be named after a saint and the first to have a clipper bow. Her first-class accommodation was aft, with cabins opening off the saloon, her second-class in the forecastle, she had no boat deck and no superstructure to speak of — all characteristic of dozens of vessels of a generation and more. In the second *St Clair,* of 1937, the first-class accommodation was for the first time amidships, with dining saloon under the bridge and ranges of cabins on two decks, and no Ladies' Cabin, and she had a superstructure far surpassing that of any earlier ship; the second-class was aft, with six- and eight-berth rooms in place of the old dormitories; she was the first of the Company's ships to have air-conditioning; initially coal-burning, she was converted to oil-burning but was the last of the Company's steamships. The third *St Clair,* of 1960, concentrated all her passenger accommodation between the main hatches and it was distributed over four decks, with public room accommodation far more spacious than any previous vessel had had. Her handsome flared bow and her tripod masts, the forward one abaft the wheelhouse, showed at a glance that she was following what had become the current fashion. The present *St Clair* (1977) is the first drive-through vessel to be placed on the Aberdeen-Lerwick route, and she is the first one-class ship on a main service. Her public rooms, including a cafeteria, are all on one deck, and most of the sleeping accommodation is also on one deck.

The withdrawal of the *St Ninian* in 1971 meant the end of the cruises to Orkney and Shetland which had so long been a feature of the Company's programme, and in the same year the St Magnus Hotel at Hillswick was sold. However, in the following year the Company introduced 'mini-cruises' to utilise some of the passenger capacity of the third *St Clair* in April-May and September-October: passengers left Aberdeen on Thursday and lived on the ship until she returned to Aberdeen on Sunday morning, and as long as the *Earl of Zetland* continued it was possible to combine a trip to the North Isles with the return passage on the *St Clair.* This innovation proved remarkably successful and met a very real need, at a time when all accommodation in Shetland was becoming over-taxed because of the oil developments, and the mini-cruises enabled many people to pay short visits to Shetland who would not otherwise have done so. In 1977, with the introduction of the fourth *St Clair,* mini-cruises were offered on the Monday-Wednesday run also, giving a twelve-hour stay in Lerwick which could be convenient for business purposes as well as for pleasure. The total number of 'mini-cruisers' therefore rose from 1339 in 1976 to 3907 in

1977. A change of time-table to extend the first return trip in the week by a day is likely to increase the number still more. It also became possible in 1977, in association with Shetland hotels, to revive what are now called 'sail and stay' holidays, offering the return trip on the ship plus a week in Shetland.

As it turned out, the withdrawal from Leith in 1971 was not permanent. In four years or a little more the Company was back at Leith with a cargo service, carried on by various P. & O. cargo vessels, especially the *Ortolan,* and then by the *Rof Beaver,* a vehicle-carrying ship which frequently proceeded to the oil centre at Sullom Voe. What was happening, of course, was that the oil developments enormously increased the demand for transport to the islands. Nor was the 'North Company' — or rather P. & O. — alone in this field. The Company had never, indeed, had anything like a complete monopoly of cargo, but now other lines began to advertise regular, scheduled, cargo services. The figures for cargo and livestock carried by P. & O. in 1976, if compared with the figures in chapter 4, suggest that the Company had lost some ground: feeding-stuffs 7635 tons, fertiliser 4429 tons, frozen fish 2883 tons, fresh fish 467 tons, whisky 1811 tons, cattle 29,837 and sheep 76,230. These statistics must, however, be considered in the light of various changes in the economic emphasis in the islands, especially in Shetland.

The latest challenge has come, not surprisingly, from a concern operating, under the name Orkney and Shetland Carriers, a vehicle-carrying ship from Scrabster to Stromness and Sandwick (half way between Lerwick and Sumburgh). The use of Scrabster as a terminal point on the Scottish mainland is by no means a novel idea, but it involves a very long haul by road or rail from central Scotland or further south, for the sake of a relatively modest shortening of the sea-passage (less than 40%). It is interesting that in 1907 the *Norseman* was advertised as providing the 'shortest sea journey to Shetland — Wick to Lerwick every Tuesday evening — 11 hours'. Thus does history repeat itself.

REFERENCE

1 See Chapter 5.

19. *St Sunniva (II)*

20. *St Clair (II)*, later *St Magnus (IV)*

21. *St Fergus*

22. *St Clement (I)*

23. *St Clement (II)*

24. *St Rognvald (III)*

PART II

THE SHIPS

G

THE SHIPS[1]

The variety of vessels employed by the North of Scotland Company and its predecessors and successors over the years has been manifold, but there were certain characteristics about which it is possible to generalise. Hulls have almost invariably been black, with white topsides, but the *St Sunniva* (II) was entirely white and the *St Fergus* and *St Clement* (I) were grey. It seems that the *St Magnus* (I) had a grey hull at one stage, probably near the end of her career. Deck-house exteriors were of wood in the older vessels and in the *St Sunniva* (II), and when metal took the place of wood, as it did from the *St Ninian* (I), the metal was oak-grained until 1937, when white paint was substituted. At the same time, the lifeboats, previously grained and varnished, were also painted white.

For long, the standard funnel colour was black, but the *St Rognvald* (I) and *St Sunniva* (I) had yellow funnels in their cruising days.[2] The *St Sunniva* (I), after a spell of black when she was transferred to the Aberdeen-Lerwick service in 1909, reverted after the First World War to yellow, which she shared for a year or two with the *St Margaret* (II). The second *St Sunniva* of course had a yellow funnel, and in 1937, when the second *St Clair* appeared with a yellow funnel, the *St Magnus* (III) and *St Rognvald* (II), but not the older ships, were brought into line. All ships built for the Company in and after 1937 had yellow funnels, but the *Amelia* retained her black-topped yellow funnel and the *Rora Head* had a black funnel.

The open bridge was invariable until after the First World War, but at that time wheelhouses were erected on all the existing vessels except the *Earl of Zetland* (I), and they have of course formed part of the original structure of all vessels from the *St Magnus* (III) onwards; the *Amelia,* later acquired by the Company, retained her open bridge to the end. All ships before the *St Rognvald* (II) had uncovered poop-decks, and among later ships the *St Giles* (II), *St Margaret* (I), *St Magnus* (II) and *St Sunniva* (II), as well as the acquired *St Catherine* (I), adhered to the older pattern. On some such vessels awnings could be erected over the after deck to give shelter to passengers — certainly on the *St Nicholas, St Clair* (I), *St Magnus* (II), *St Sunniva* (I) and (II) and *St Ninian* (I). The *St Rognvald* (II) was the first ship with a promenade deck extending right to the stern.

With few exceptions, the passenger ships have for a long time been designed and equipped for handling cargo on the starboard side only, and this arrangement always resulted in a certain saving of deck space. The North Isles of Shetland steamers, however, were designed to work mainly on the port side, and as Scalloway was worked on that side some vessels on the west-side service were equipped for port-side working. The preference from quite an early date was for the handier free-standing and power-rotated crane rather than a derrick or boom on the mast, and when the *St Catherine* (I) was acquired in 1930 cranes were soon installed and the booms removed. The North Isles and cargo vessels, however, have been exceptions to this rule. Some at least of the earlier ships had wells both fore and aft, but most later passenger ships had a well forward and a trunk hatch aft, though the first and second *St Sunniva* each had trunks both fore and aft. The *St Magnus* (III), *St Clair* (II) and *St Clair* (III) each had two hatches forward and one aft, the *St Ninian* (II), with her short fore deck, had one hatch forward and two aft. The older vessels had open 'tween-deck space. The *St Clair* (I) may have had nothing else throughout her long career, and the *St Catherine* (I) retained this arrangement, so suitable for the carriage of stock. Reference was made in chapter 4 to the practice of sealing off the passenger accommodation amidships on the main deck in some vessels; but that area could also be opened up from the forward end to create a spacious 'tween-decks.

Until the First War most if not all of the ships carried sails which were sometimes handy to facilitate manoeuvring, and which were also used, as an inexpensive form of stabilisers, to check rolling.

In ships before the second *St Clair,* first-class accommodation was aft, second-class accommodation forward. The *St Clair* (II) conformed to what had become the usual practice in other lines, by concentrating first-class accommodation between the main hatches and placing second-class accommodation aft. This, however, was a passing fashion, for the *St Ninian* (II) and *St Clair* (III) had no passenger accommodation towards either bows or stern, but, by a curious reversion to earlier practice, the second-class accommodation was again forward of the first-class.

In nearly all passenger vessels before the second *St Clair* the settees in the public rooms could be converted into double berths, an arrangement which made the sleeping accommodation remarkably elastic and gave the *St Magnus* (III), in particular, an astounding sleeping capacity. (It should be said that until after the Second War no charges were made for sleeping-berths, and this meant that a passage fare entitled a passenger to a berth if one could be provided at all.) Electric lighting appeared, probably for the first time, on the *St Sunniva* (I), when it was evidently a novelty, and most of the older ships had it installed subsequently; but all ships down to the *St Magnus* (III) were fully equipped with paraffin lamps for use in emergencies, and the ornate hanging lamps in the saloon gave the ship an old-world air. The abandonment, with the *St Magnus* (III), of the more or less horse-shoe shaped dining saloon in the stern deprived the captain of an obvious place of honour at the head of a long table, where he had presided over the company, and although the *St Sunniva* (II) reverted to the dining saloon right aft the layout was of a number of small tables; a similar arrangement of tables has continued in all later ships. A piano had been a common piece of furniture in passenger ships even before the days of steam, and may well have been introduced to North of Scotland ships before the *St Rognvald* (I), when a piano is first mentioned; a piano of good quality remained a standard item of equipment in all ships before the *St Clair* (II). The instrument was not very frequently used, but some travellers remember how the late Captain Stout, after he had taken the *St Magnus* (III) out of Lerwick on a Sunday evening, would settle down at the piano in the saloon and lead passengers in community hymn-singing. The piano returned on the fourth *St Clair,* although in very different surroundings from the staid old dining saloons where pianos used to be.

The fourth *St Clair* represents other breaks with tradition. The hand-bell with which stewards used to summon passengers to meals was, so far as I know, a feature of all previous ships except the second *St Sunniva,* where a steward paraded the decks with a gong instead. The once familiar sound of the bell — like the sounds associated with the days of steam — has now vanished. It is perhaps significant of the attachment to the bell that the third *St Clair* inherited the bell of the second *St Rognvald* and on the sale of the *St Clair* this bell, connected as it is with two very distinguished ships, has found a place in the Lerwick Museum. Another bell that was familiar was the main bell on the fore-deck, which used to give the signal of readiness to sail. The first *St Sunniva's* bell happened to be recovered from the seabed about forty years after her loss and it also has been placed in the Museum, where the main bell of the third *St Clair* will be its neighbour.

Larger ships and growing numbers of passengers led in the end to a break with a tradition which some thought had survived too long. While passengers arriving on board have for many years checked their accommodation with the chief steward and have been shown to their rooms by a steward or stewardess, the whole business of checking tickets and the sale of tickets to those who did not have them before coming on board was handled by the purser and the chief officer as they toured the ship. It was an elaborate operation, necessitating stationing stewards at various points to prevent passengers escaping the net. And to have money, and especially banknotes, passing from hand to hand on an open deck on a breezy day always seemed risky. But there was an old-world air and a personal touch about the procedure which is not now represented in the same way.

Reference was made in chapter 2 to the practice of naming the ships after saints, beginning with the *St Magnus* in 1867. This has continued ever since, except that the time-honoured name of *Earl of Zetland* (not originally bestowed by the North of Scotland Company) was retained for the new North Isles steamer in 1939 and that some cargo ships acquired from other owners did not become 'Saints'. The reasons lying behind the selection of the saints' names may not be immediately obvious, and an enquirer who consults a collection of *Lives of the Saints* is as likely to be mystified as to be enlightened. He will not readily learn why ships trading in northern waters should commemorate St Clair, St Clement, St Giles or St Nicholas, for example. St Clair is believed to have been a native of Rochester who became a hermit in Normandy in the Dark Ages and was assassinated at the instigation of a high-born lady whose advances he had repulsed, but there may also have been another St Clair in Normandy in somewhat later times, and from one or other of those saints places in France took their names. The best-known (though not the only) St Clement is mentioned in the New Testament (Philippians, iv, 3) as a fellow-worker of St Paul; he became the second or third Bishop of Rome and, so it said, met his end about the year 100 in the Crimea, where he was thrown into the sea with an anchor round his neck. St Giles was a hermit in the south of France early in the eighth century. The most famous St Nicholas was an archbishop of Myra in Asia Minor who came to be regarded as the patron saint of sailors but is best remembered as the patron saint of children, and his name was corrupted into the familiar Santa Claus. All of those figures seem sufficiently remote from the North of Scotland, Orkney and Shetland.

Yet a very real link, and a very sound explanation, does exist in those and other cases, and the names of the ships have for the most part been intelligently chosen. Most of the names, especially those which have persisted from one generation to another, have had some association with the ports which the ships served. Outstanding are the names of St Magnus and St Rognvald, for these men were Earls of Orkney when the earldom included Shetland as well as Orkney, and it was Rognvald who built, in honour of his uncle, Magnus, the great church in Kirkwall which was the cathedral for both groups of islands. The principal church in Shetland, at Tingwall, was also dedicated to St Magnus. Those two names are therefore peculiarly suited to ships serving both Orkney and Shetland. The relevance of the name 'St Clair' does not arise directly from the saint. From a place in Normandy called 'St Clair' there came to Scotland in the thirteenth century William of St Clair, who acquired the lands of Roslin. He was the founder of 'the lordly line of high St Clair' who for a time ruled Orkney as earls but had a much longer association with Caithness: indeed, Sinclair remained the name of the Earls of Caithness until 1911. This was therefore a very appropriate name for a ship serving the Caithness ports of Wick and Thurso, and few ships have ever been more fittingly named than the first *St Clair,* which was associated with the run to Caithness throughout nearly all her long career. (It must be said, by contrast, that few ships have been as unsuitably named — from the historical point of view —

as the third and fourth *St Clair,* which have never called at a port anywhere near Caithness.) The connection of St Ninian with the islands and with the north of Scotland is more shadowy, although, while his sphere of work was centred in the south-west of Scotland, there are dedications to him right up the east coast, and the place-name St Ninian's Isle occurs in Shetland. Leith also had a church dedicated to St Ninian. When the choice of this name was first made for a ship, in 1895, it justified itself, for the first *St Ninian* had a singularly trouble-free life of fifty years. On the second *St Ninian* the saint was commemorated on an engraved panel on the main stairway. The beautiful name *St Sunniva* was a most felicitous choice. This saint was an Irish princess who fled to Norway to escape from a brutal neighbour but ran into trouble there as well, and she and her followers, so it is related, prayed that rocks might fall on them and kill them, because they feared nature less than man. The place of her death was the island of Selja, but her relics were later taken to Bergen cathedral. Her shrine there was partly maintained by revenues sent from Shetland, and there was a dedication to St Sunniva in Shetland itself, on the island of Balta. This name, therefore, was very suitable for a ship cruising to Norway, and not unsuitable for a ship on the direct run to Shetland. It was appropriate that for some years her partner on the direct run between Leith and Shetland was the *St Giles,* for the saint of that name was the patron saint of Edinburgh. The name St Olaf, given to the first North of Scotland steamer on the Pentland Firth crossing, is that of a king of Norway, to whom the first church in Kirkwall was dedicated; but in the local form, St Ola, it is the name of the parish in which Kirkwall and Scapa are situated, and this form was very properly preferred for the *St Olaf's* three successors. Other saints whose names were used were connected with ports on the Scottish mainland from which the ships operated. St Nicholas and St Clement had churches in Aberdeen dedicated to them, St Nicholas had a church dedicated to him in Leith as well, and St Fergus was an eighth-century bishop associated with Buchan and the Moray Firth. There was never much to be said for St Margaret as a name for a North of Scotland ship, for that lady was an English princess who became Queen of Scotland in the days when Caithness, Orkney and Shetland did not form part of the Scottish realm; however, the place-name St Margaret's Hope occurs in Orkney. There seems to have been little historical foundation for the introduction of the name St Catherine, though there were several saints so called and there were minor dedications to that name in both Aberdeen and Orkney.

It is not always easy to understand why some names persisted while others did not, though it must be emphasised that a shipping company does not have complete freedom of choice, since a name that it wants to revive may meantime have been appropriated by another firm. One can see that St Giles can hardly have been considered a lucky name, for the first ship of that name was wrecked after only ten years' service and the second was sold after another ten years. Equally, both the first and second *St Sunniva* were lost — the second of them, admittedly, in wartime — but the name was associated with a type of vessel which we shall never see again and the decision to lay it aside can hardly be challenged. On the other hand, the *St Nicholas* had a career of forty-three years before she was wrecked, and one would have expected that name to be repeated. It is odd, too, that the patron saint of Leith — St Mary — and the patron saint of Old Aberdeen — St Machar — have never been commemorated in North of Scotland ships, but the latter name was given to Aberdeen tugs.

It is relevant to any discussion of the naming of the ships that most of the main-service vessels have changed their routes over the years and that some of them have been maids-of-all work. Specialisation was most conspicuous on the direct run: the first and second *St Giles* and the first *St Margaret,* which were built for this service, set something of a precedent, for the *St Sunniva* (I) seldom and the *St Sunniva* (II) never appeared regularly except on the direct run, and the *St Clair* (III) fitted into the same pattern. The successive *St Rognvalds* were almost as rigidly confined to the indirect service, and each successive *St Magnus* also served mainly on the indirect service. Most of the other main-service ships, while they may have been more associated with one run or another, were more versatile. Apart from the main-service vessels there was, of course, more specialisation. The North Isles and Pentland Firth steamers seldom deviated from the routes for which they were designed, and the cargo ships were not in general suitable for the main services, though the *St Clement* (I) was the regular Caithness boat in winter for many years and the *St Rognvald* (III) and *St*

Clement (II) took over the Kirkwall and Lerwick services when passenger vessels were withdrawn.

Practically all the ships used to be sufficiently all-purpose and interchangeable to be able to serve as reliefs. The nature of the trade, with its heavy passenger traffic in summer and the heavy loads of livestock in the autumn, long determined that overhauls should take place mainly in the winter months. Consequently, each winter was apt to see a good deal of interchange, as one ship after another went for overhaul.

REFERENCES

1 This section deals only with the powered ships operated by the North of Scotland Company and its predecessors. Particulars of some other vessels are given in Part 1. The many ships which were managed, but not owned, by the Company during World War II are not included, and some vessels chartered for short periods have been ignored.
2 I have an old coloured postcard, obviously dating from before World War I, showing the *St Ninian* (I) with a yellow funnel. This may not be authentic, but possibly a ship on the west side run might have been regarded as a cruising vessel and painted accordingly.

ALPHABETICAL LIST OF SHIPS

(The figures given in round brackets are those of gross
tonnage. In many cases this altered over the years,
usually by way of an increase.)

Amelia (357). A conventional coastal cargo vessel, with
engine aft, but with accommodation for a few passengers under
the bridge amidships, she was built in 1894 at Ayr. After passing
through the hands of Henry Newhouse of Norwich, R. J. Leslie
of Halifax, Nova Scotia, and the Magdalen Islands Steamship
Company of Halifax, she was owned for many years from 1920
by Cooper and Company of Kirkwall, and ran weekly from
Leith to Aberdeen and Kirkwall. The Company was absorbed by
the North of Scotland in 1940, and the *Amelia,* still with her
black-topped yellow funnel, continued on her old route until
1955, when she was taken out of service and broken up.

Argyll (224). Built in 1886 by Robert Duncan and Co.,
Glasgow, for the Argyll Steamship Company of Glasgow, she
was chartered by the North of Scotland in 1891-2 for service
on the Pentland Firth and the direct run between Aberdeen and
Lerwick. She was wrecked in 1893, shortly after resuming her
usual sailings from Glasgow to Stranraer.

Bonnie Dundee (296). A wooden paddler, built in 1837 for
Dundee and Leith Steam Packet Company, she was acquired by
the Aberdeen, Leith and Clyde Company in June 1840 and served
almost entirely between Aberdeen and Newhaven, in both
summer and winter, but occasionally went to Inverness and
Lerwick and ran to Wick in summer 1851. She was sold in
March 1853 to Maryport Steamship Company and was broken
up in January 1856.

Brilliant (159). A wooden paddler, built by Laing and Company at Dumbarton in 1821, she was acquired by the Aberdeen,

Leith and Clyde in 1826. She ran from Leith to Aberdeen in summer 1821-7, but even in 1825 she made occasional trips to Inverness and Wick and she ran from Leith to Inverness in summer 1828-38. On 12 December 1839 she ran on to Aberdeen pier on the passage from Leith and was destroyed by fire, the master losing his life.

Cape Wrath (330). A cargo vessel built at Ayr in 1900 for the Cape Steam Shipping Company of Glasgow, she was owned by the North of Scotland 1916-27. She subsequently passed to D. and J. Allen, Methil (1927-30) and the Western General Shipping Company, Glamorgan (1930-2). She was stranded in the River Severn on 21 March 1932 and, although refloated, was later broken up.

City of Aberdeen (972). On the loss of the *St Rognvald* (I), the Company chartered first the *Bear* from the Liverpool and Clyde Steam Navigation Company and then the *Ban Righ* from the Aberdeen Steam Navigation Company. The latter stranded at Cairnbulg on 25 June 1900, on her second run south, and the *City of Aberdeen* was then chartered from the Aberdeen Steam Navigation Company to serve on the weekend run.

Commodore (760). A wooden paddler chartered from the Aberdeen Steam Navigation Company and operated by the Aberdeen, Leith and Clyde from Leith to Lerwick and to Inverness in 1857-8, after the loss of the *Queen* (I).

Duke of Richmond (497). A wooden paddler, built on the Clyde by John Wood in 1838, she was lengthened by 12 feet by A. Hall and Co., Aberdeen, in 1843. She ran from Leith to Wick, Kirkwall and Lerwick at the end of 1838 and in summer 1853-7. She was, however, mainly associated with the Inverness run, for she was on it in summer 1838-52 and in winter 1849-52. She latterly ran from Leith to Wick, in the winters of 1852-9 and in the summers of 1858 and 1859. On 8 October 1859, when on passage from Wick to Aberdeen, she ran ashore 1½ miles from the mouth of the River Don and became a total loss.

Duke of Rothesay (578). Chartered from the Aberdeen Steam Navigation Company for the sailings from Leith to Inverness in the summer of 1858.

Dundee (638). A wooden paddler chartered from the Dundee, Perth and London Company for sailings from Leith to Wick in April 1863 and to Lerwick in May 1863, to replace the *Prince Consort.*

Dunleary (480). A coastal collier, built at Glasgow in 1905 for W. O. McCormick and Company, Dublin. After passing through the hands of the Holden S. S. Company, Fowey (1932-6) and the Arran Shipping Company of Irvine (1936-40), she was acquired by the North of Scotland in 1940 and retained by them until 1947, when she was sold to Milton Zagrafos, Piraeus, and renamed *Georgios Z* and later *Floga.* As *Sofia,* she foundered off the coast of Cyrenaica on 17 September 1962.

Earl of Aberdeen (820). An iron paddler, chartered from the Aberdeen Steam Navigation Company in 1857-8 for sailings from Leith to Lerwick and Inverness.

Earl of Zetland (I) (186/253).[1] Built by J. Fullerton and Co., Paisley, in 1877, for the Shetland Islands Steam Navigation Company, Lerwick, she was lengthened by 23 feet in the early months of 1884 and then measured 144.8 feet by 20 feet of beam. She was taken over by the North of Scotland in 1890. Throughout her long career her station was Lerwick and she was employed almost entirely on the North Isles and Yellsound services, but down to 1914 she ran frequently to the south Mainland of Shetland as well, she was regular relief vessel on the Pentland Firth for many years, and in the days before the First War, both before and after being acquired by the North of Scotland, she made occasional trips to Leith and Aberdeen. In 1886 she took part in the search for the smack *Columbine* when that vessel had started on the remarkable drift, with only Elizabeth Mouat on board, which ultimately took her to Norway. Before her lengthening, she had wells both fore and aft, but afterwards the after well was eliminated and the after hatch not used on her normal services. Apart from the lengthening, she underwent few alterations, but at the end of 1930 the rails round the bridge and the flying bridge were replaced by teak boarding, and during the Second War, when she was protectively armed, she acquired a wheelhouse. Among other mishaps, she was ashore on Lunna Holm on 26 July 1912 and on Robbie Ramsay's Baa on 28 August 1924. Renamed *Earl of Zetland II* in 1939, when the launching of her successor was imminent, she served under that name through the war years. She was attacked by enemy aircraft in May and October 1941. Withdrawn from service in 1946, she was sold to the Anal Compania Provential S.A., Panama, and renamed *Anal* with a view to running illegal immigrants into Palestine. Under the name *Yehuda Halevy,* she was arrested by the British Navy in 1947 and beached at Haifa; she was broken up in 1950.

Earl of Zetland (II) (548). The first motor vessel owned by North of Scotland Company, she was built by Hall, Russell and Co., Aberdeen, and brought into service at the end of August 1939. Of dimensions 154.9 ft. by 29.1 ft., her additional tonnage, as compared with her predecessor, was due mainly to her greater beam, for shallow draught was an advantage in her work. In her general layout she followed the well-tried lines of the first *Earl,* with a well surrounding the hatch (forward), for convenience in working with flitboats, and no after-hatch. Her passenger accommodation was, naturally, much superior, with dining saloon and smoking room on the upper deck, aft, an enclosed observation compartment under the bridge, and accommodation for a considerable number of passengers in two-berth cabins on the main and lower decks. Originally, second-class accommodation was provided forward, but later she became a one-class ship. During the Second World War this vessel was on special service on the Pentland Firth, where she steamed over 100,000 miles and carried some 600,000 persons. In 1945 she made some Aberdeen-Kirkwall runs, was then restored to the service for which she had been designed and also relieved the *St Ola* on the Pentland Firth and made an occasional trip to Aberdeen. Her service with the North of Scotland finished at the end of February 1975, after which she was acquired by Middlesbrough Ocean Surveys and named *Celtic Surveyor.*

Express (217). Built at South Shields in 1869 for George Robertson's Pentland Firth service, she served after 1877 between Kirkwall and Scottish ports.[2] Originally of 121 gross tons, she was lengthened by 35 feet in 1882. In 1896 she was sold to other Kirkwall owners, and from 1898 was running weekly between Leith and Kirkwall *via* Aberdeen. Acquired by the North of Scotland in 1917, she was lost in collision off the French coast on 4 April of that year.

Fetlar (I) (467). Built in 1898 as the *Ape*, a cargo steamer for the Greenock-Belfast service of G. and J. Burns, she was sold in 1912 to H. Newhouse and Co., Yarmouth, and in 1916 to Cunningham, Shaw and Co., who sold her to the North of Scotland in 1918. She sank on 13 April 1919 after striking Bunel Rock, St Malo Roads.

Fetlar (II) (369). Built in 1883 as the *Cavalier* for David MacBrayne's service from Glasgow to Inverness *via* the Caledonian Canal, she occasionally served as a relief on the Glasgow-Islay and Glasgow-Stornoway routes, as well as from Glasgow to Greenock. She was acquired by the North of Scotland in 1919, and among other duties she relieved on the North Isles service. She was sold in March 1920 to the Dundalk and Newry Steam Packet Company and was broken up in 1927.[3]

Hamburg (693). An iron paddler, built at Govan in 1849, she was sold after three years to Grimsby owners, but was re-acquired by the Aberdeen, Leith and Clyde in 1860. From 1860 to 1862 she ran from Leith to Caithness in both summer and winter, with occasional extensions to Kirkwall and to Stornoway. She was wrecked on Scotston Head, 12 October 1862.

Highlander (1216). A passenger and cargo steamer, built in 1916 for the Aberdeen, Newcastle and Hull Shipping Company, and regularly employed on service among those ports, she was acquired by the North of Scotland in October 1939, after the requisitioning of the *St Sunniva* (II), *St Magnus* (III) and *St Ninian* (I). On 1 August 1940, while on passage from Aberdeen to Leith, she was attacked by German aircraft 10 miles S.S.E. of Girdleness, but brought down two of the hostile planes and steamed into Leith with the wreckage of one of them on her poop. The deed well deserved recognition, and Captain William Gifford and two of the crew were decorated, but the achievement received a degree of publicity in the press and wireless which some rightly deplored and which was fatal in the end to the *Highlander*. She was marked out for vengeance, and, despite being re-named *St Catherine* (II) and surviving two more aerial attacks, on 13 and 18-19 September, she was sunk on 14 November 1940 off Aberdeen. Captain J. G. Norquay, thirteen members of the crew, and one passenger, were lost; three passengers and fourteen of the crew were rescued.

Newhaven (259). A wooden paddler, built for the Brighton and Continental Steam Packet Company in 1847, she was the property of the Aberdeen, Leith and Clyde from May 1849 to August 1851 and was employed between Leith and Aberdeen in summer. She was sold to William Geach, London, and disappeared from the register after 1886.

Nigel (280). Chartered in the winter of 1891-2 for the direct run, carrying mails and cargo only. She was owned successively by W. McLachlan and Company (1886-91), A. F. Blackater (1891-5) and K. Cameron, Junior (1895) — all of Glasgow.

Oscar (806). Chartered from the London and Edinburgh Shipping Company and employed briefly by the Aberdeen, Leith and Clyde in the summer of 1867.

Prince Consort (623). An iron paddler, she was built for the Aberdeen, Leith and Clyde at Port Glasgow, and made her first trip to Lerwick on 27 March 1858. She was on the Leith-Lerwick run in summer from 1858 to 1867 and in winter from 1859 to 1861, and on the Leith-Wick run in the winter of 1862-3; she made a run to London in February 1862. She was aground at Noss Head on 18 September 1860 and in 1863 she struck the North Pier at Aberdeen. After the latter accident she was bought by Messrs. Cato, Thomson and Company, who reconstructed her 'on the most approved principles' and then re-sold her to the Aberdeen, Leith and Clyde. On the morning of Saturday, 11 May 1867, after leaving Leith for Aberdeen at 7 p.m. on Friday, she ran aground in fog on the Allten Rock, opposite the village of Burnbanks, north of Cove. She broke in three pieces and went down in half an hour, but there was no loss of life. Throughout most of her career, the *Prince Consort* was commanded by Captain Parrott.[4]

Queen (I) (328). A wooden paddler, built in 1845, she was employed between Leith and Inverness in summer 1845-7 and

25. *St Olaf*

26. *St Ola (I)*

27. *Amelia*

28. *St Ola (II)*

29. *Earl of Zetland (I)*

30. *Earl of Zetland (II)*

1853-6, and also in winter 1852-7; she ran from Leith to Lerwick in summer 1848-52 and from Leith to Wick in winter 1851-2. She struck the Carr Rock on 19 April 1857, while on passage from Aberdeen to Leith, and, although beached at Crail, she broke up in a gale on 25 April and became a total loss.

Queen (II) (448). An iron screw steamer with a compound engine, she was built at Port Glasgow in 1861. Her first duty was the winter run to Lerwick, which she carried out from 1861 to 1870. In summer, she at first served from time to time on the Caithness run, but when the second summer run to Shetland was started she took it on from 1866 to 1871. Throughout most of the 1870s she was on various duties. These included several voyages to Iceland in 1872-3; these were mainly for ponies, but in August 1873 it was reported that she had brought to Leith 160 emigrants who proceeded to Glasgow on their way to Quebec. She was on the briefly revived Inverness service in 1874 and Caithness for part of the summer of 1878, and in winter 1875-6 she was operated by the Aberdeen Steam Navigation Company. Then, just as she had pioneered the successful winter sailings to Shetland and the second summer run, so she was chosen in the summer of 1881 to pioneer the west-side service, while in the winter of 1881-2 she operated the second winter sailing to Shetland when it was introduced. From 1882 to 1898 and again from 1907 to 1911 she was the usual winter boat for the west side, and she served on that route during at least part of several summers between 1886 and 1898. It is mainly as a west-side boat that she is remembered. Yet she was from time to time employed elsewhere — Kirkwall and Lerwick in 1889, the Pentland Firth in 1890 and 1892, the direct service in the winter of 1902-3 (after the loss of the *St Giles* (I)), Caithness in the winter of 1906-7. Her last notable service was in the summer of 1907, when she ran from Leith to Aberdeen to provide a connection with the direct boat — and in this she was again in a sense a pioneer. However, from the late 1890s much of her time was taken up in relief duties and outside runs. She was sold in 1911 to P. C. Marretto, Constantinople, and renamed *Amalia;* in 1917 she was sold to A. de Media, Leghorn, and, after being seized at Sebastopol during the Russian Revolution, she was broken up.

H

Rof Beaver (963). Built at Elmshorn, Germany, in 1971 as *Bibiana,* but re-named *Irish Fame* before she was commissioned, then *Monarch Fame* in 1972, *Bibiana* (again) in 1973, *Helga One* and finally *Rof Beaver* in 1975. A freight-vehicle carrier, she served from Leith to Orkney and Shetland, especially Sullom Voe and Lerwick.

Rora Head (492). A conventional coastal cargo steamer, built in Southampton for the General Steam Navigation Company, London, in 1921, as the *Blackcock,* she passed through the hands of Comben Longstaff and Co. as the *Brooktown* and was acquired in 1937 by A. F. Henry and Macgregor of Leith, who named her *Rora Head.* The North of Scotland bought her in 1939. After the Second World War she generally operated the cargo service to Caithness as long as it continued, but she was sold in 1956 to Hay and Company, Lerwick.

St Catherine (I) (1,065). Built in 1893, as the *Olive,* for Alexander A. Laird and Company's Glasgow-Londonderry run, she was originally of 1,141 tons and had accommodation for 100 saloon passengers and 1,000 steerage passengers. Later some of the accommodation was removed and the tonnage reduced to 1,047 and she ran from Heysham to Londonderry. On the amalgamation of the Burns and Laird fleets in 1929 she was renamed *Lairdsbank,* and in 1930 was sold to the North of Scotland after the loss of the *St Sunniva* (I). She served, in the emergency, on the west side in the summer of 1930, but, with sleeping accommodation for only about sixty first-class passengers, she was quite inadequate for any of the Company's summer services, and thereafter she was laid up each summer but served very acceptably on the direct run in winter until 1937 and made very occasional appearances on indirect services. Described as 'a beautiful vessel', she had in truth a handsome profile, she was well-powered for her size, and she had a good reputation as a sea boat. She was conspicuous for her length (260 ft.), which made her 30 ft. longer than the *St Rognvald* (II), of similar tonnage, and 10 ft. longer than the much larger *St Magnus* (III). The North of Scotland made few alterations except the substitution of cranes for the booms on the masts and the erection of a small deck shelter forward of the after hold.

With staterooms opening off the dining saloon, which had a single long table, she was an old-fashioned vessel even for her age. She was sold for breaking-up at Rosyth in 1937.

St Catherine (11), *see* **Highlander.**

St Clair (1) (641). An iron screw steamer, built at Govan, of dimensions 205.6 ft. by 26.6 ft., she arrived at Aberdeen under Captain Angus on 29 March 1868, and made her first trip to Wick, the port with which she was always to be mainly associated, returning on 10 April. She served the Caithness ports in summer, with little intermission, year by year until 1914 and again from 1920 to 1936, and in winter from 1868 to 1871, in 1875, from 1886 to 1914 and from 1921 to 1925. Next to Caithness, her associations were with the west side. She was there during part of the summer in 1883 to 1887 and in 1919; and in winter she served on this arduous route from 1891 to 1914 and again, after World War I, until almost her end. She was no stranger to the indirect run on the east side, but her periods of service there were mostly brief. On 19 January 1918 she was attacked by a submarine off Fair Isle and two of her company were killed, but she returned the enemy fire and it was believed that she sank the attacker. Originally the *St Clair* had no after deckhouse, she had wells at both hatches and had gaffs on both masts. Later, she had a gaff and a well only forward, and for a time, booms as well as cranes. After the War, she was re-engined and modernised to the extent of having patent davits fitted for her four boats, but otherwise she underwent little permanent alteration. With her clipper bow, her deck flush from the poop to the bridge and no boat deck, she was in her later years a visible link with the past. Internally, too, with her staterooms opening off the dining saloon, she had an antique appearance. Yet, being completely free from top-hamper and having her limited cargo capacity usually well filled, she had a reputation of being a good sea boat, and her new engines gave her a fair turn of speed. To the end she was not the least useful member of the fleet. In 1936, in preparation for the launching of her successor, she was renamed *St Colm,* and ran for a few months on outside duties. In 1937 she was sold for breaking up in Germany.[4a]

St Clair (II) (1,637). The Company's last steamship, she was the first to depart from the long-established pattern which so many vessels had followed, for her first-class accommodation was concentrated amidships, with dining saloon under the bridge and a glassed-in promenade at the forward end of the boat deck, while the second-class accommodation was aft and consisted of smaller rooms in place of the old open dormitories. With an overall length of 267 feet and a breadth of 38, she was also the largest ship yet built, slightly exceeding the dimensions of the *St Magnus* (III). Built and brought into use in 1937, she operated until 1939 on the west side in summer and the weekend run in winter. In 1940 she was requisitioned, and as H.M.S. *Baldur* took part in the British occupation of Iceland; later she was a rescue ship. In 1945-6 she was refitted and converted to oil-burning. From 1946 to 1960 she served on the direct run between Aberdeen and Lerwick, and from the summer of 1960, when she was renamed first *St Clair II* and then *St Magnus* (IV), she was on the weekend run in summer and part of the winter but also relieved her successor on the direct run. This last of the passenger steamships made her final voyage from Lerwick to Leith on 30 March - 1 April 1967. She was finally renamed *St Magnus II* before being sold to Van Heyghen Frères for demolition.

St Clair (III) (3302/2864). A motor vessel, launched at Troon on 29 February 1960 and appointed to the direct run in both summer and winter, she was far the largest of the Company's ships to date and included many improvements and refinements which were a striking commentary on the progress in ship design within a generation. With a length of 297 feet and a beam of 49, she was a massive ship, with passenger accommodation on four decks, spacious public rooms, three cargo hatches and chill and refrigerated space. The superstructure was of aluminium, and she was the first of the Company's ships to be fitted with anti-roll stabilisers. During one winter she served as a relief on the Irish Sea. She left Lerwick on her last normal trip on 2 April 1977, but she returned, rather unexpectedly, to Victoria Pier with cargo a fortnight later and made two or three runs after that until June. She was then sold to the Meat and Foodstuff Company of Kuwait and renamed *Al Khairat*.

St Clair (IV) (4468). Built at Lübeck as *Peter Pan* 1964 and operated between Oslo and Århus; as *Panther* operated for Southern Ferries from Southampton to San Sebastian 1973-5 and as *Terje Vigen* again between Oslo and Århus 1976; re-named *St Clair* and took service between Aberdeen and Lerwick 4 April 1977. She is 402 feet long, with beam of 57 feet.

St Clement (I) (450).[5] A cargo steamer, with engine room aft and accommodation for twelve passengers under the bridge amidships, she was built for the Company in 1928. In general appearance her profile closely resembled that of the *St Fergus* but she was most readily identifiable by a mizzen mast which the *St Fergus* did not have. In winter, down to 1939, she served regularly on the Caithness run, and each autumn she relieved the *Earl of Zetland* (I) in the North Isles. While she was engaged on the latter duty, she ran ashore in Saltwick, on the east coast of Yell, in heavy rain on 18 October 1928 and received considerable damage, but was able to proceed to Aberdeen under her own steam. In summer she was an outside boat, carrying various cargoes, shipping livestock from the islands and, in the height of the herring season, carrying herring from Lerwick to Germany. She was sunk in an air attack on 5 April 1941, twenty miles south-east of Peterhead, and the chief engineer was lost.

St Clement (II) (815). A motor vessel with the same general character as her predecessor, she was built by Hall, Russell and Co. in 1946. After one season (the summer of 1955), when she ran to Wick and Thurso, her regular run until 1966 was that from Leith to Kirkwall and Stromness, which she shared with the *St Rognvald* (III); when calls at Stromness ceased she continued to run regularly to Kirkwall for most of each year. She relieved the *St Ola* on the Pentland Firth and from the summer of 1966 to that of 1974 supplemented her on that service. She made one trip to Hillswick, when the hotel there was re-fitted after the Second War. For a time she relieved in the North Isles of Shetland, but that duty later fell to the *St Ola* (II). She was sold at the end of 1976 to E. G. Loukedes, Greece, who re-named her *Grigoris*.

St Colm, *see* **St Clair** (I).

St Fergus (390).[6] The first cargo vessel ordered for the Company, she was built by Hawthorns of Leith in 1913 but was sold before delivery to the New Patagonian Meat and Cold Storage Company, Buenos Aires, and bought back in 1916. Of conventional type, she resembled the *St Clement* (I), but had no passenger accommodation. Her only regular service was on the Caithness run for parts of the winters in the 1920s, before the building of the *St Clement,* and her main work was as an outside boat. She survived an attack by a German bomber on 29 November 1940, but was sunk in collision with the *Fidra* off Rattray Head on 31 December 1940, and her master, Captain Toman, was lost.

St Giles (I) (407). Built in 1892 for the direct Aberdeen - Lerwick service, she was employed on it, both summer and winter, throughout her career. She ran ashore near Rattray Head lighthouse in fog on her passage south on 28 September 1902, was at once severely holed and, hanging on two rocks, broke her back. Originally 161 ft. by 25 ft. by 12 ft., she was lengthened by 23 ft. to cope with growing traffic and this increased her tonnage to 465.

St Giles (II) (609). Built in 1903, she served, as her namesake had done, on the direct run, in both summer and winter, until 1912. She was sold in 1913 to the government of Zanzibar and, renamed *Psyche* and later *Khalifa,* she was used as a yacht by the Sultan; she was broken up in 1928. It is clear that her plan represented a desire to make additional arrangements for the comfort and convenience of passengers, for there was accommodation for them on the upper deck amidships and, although she did not follow the *St Rognvald* of 1901 in having a promenade deck aft, there was space available for passengers on the boat deck, aft of the navigating bridge. Yet she does not seem to have been a particularly popular ship, and the only explanation of her sale, after only ten years' service, is that she had not been a success. She was ashore on Mousa on 17 October 1904.

St Magnus (I) (618).[7] An iron paddler, built in 1864 for the North British Railway Company as the *Waverley,* for the Silloth-Belfast service, she was acquired by the Aberdeen, Leith and Clyde in 1867. She was the last paddler, and the only two-funnelled vessel, owned by the Company. Her service was almost entirely confined to Leith-Aberdeen-Kirkwall-Lerwick, either as the secondary indirect boat or on the weekend run (where she relieved the *St Rognvald* (1) when the latter went cruising). She appears almost continuously on one or other of those routes, summer by summer, from 1867 to 1901, though latterly in only the early part of each season. She sometimes relieved the *St Giles* (I) on the direct run, but was rarely if at all used on any regular run in winter. This ship lives in memory, or rather in legend, as a flier, and was said to have been originally designed for blockade-running during the American Civil War: it was sometimes asserted that she held the record for the direct run between Aberdeen and Lerwick until the advent of the *St Clair* (III). But there is little evidence to support such a claim, and on the whole it seems unlikely that she could match the 16 knots claimed for the *St Sunniva* (I). The legend may originate in the fact that in August 1875 she made the passage from Lerwick to Kirkwall in 7 hours 16 minutes, which, if not a record, was uncommonly smart. She was sold in 1904 to L. F. Imossi, Gibraltar, and re-named *Magnus;* she was broken up at Rotterdam in 1913.

St Magnus (II) (809/957). Built in 1912 by Ramage and Ferguson, Leith, she measured 215 feet by 31, had accommodation for 150 first-class and 100 second-class passengers and attained the speed of 14.2 knots on her trials. She was considered a good sea-boat, but was obviously not designed for the leading services of the Company and during her very brief peacetime career she was the secondary indirect boat in summer (1913, 1914), while in the winter of 1913-4 she served partly on the Stromness and Lerwick run and partly on the Caithness run. About noon on 12 February 1918, while on passage direct from Lerwick to Aberdeen, she was sunk by enemy action off Peterhead. The weather was fine, and the crew and passengers got away in two of the boats, with the exception of two passengers and a member of the engine-room staff who was on watch below and had no chance to escape. The boats were picked up by a mine-sweeper and taken into Peterhead.

St Magnus (III) (1591). Built in 1924, with dimensions 250 ft.

by 36, she was far the largest ship yet built for the Company
and was a very roomy vessel. Her beam was sufficient to
compensate for her considerable top-weight, and, after the
inevitable prejudice against a vessel of her height had been
overcome, she earned a deserved reputation as a good sea-boat.
She was the first of the Company's vessels to have three hatches,
but despite her greater size her plan was essentially that of the
St Rognvald (II). However, her navigating bridge was raised
above the boat deck, making the whole of the latter available
for first-class passengers, and the forward end of that deck was
(though not originally) enclosed with glass panels. Internally,
the winter dining saloon was no longer right aft, but adjacent
to the summer dining saloon. Staterooms, including a number
on the upper deck, were four-berth, and the smokingroom was
under the bridge. The permanent accommodation included the
traditional Ladies' Cabin aft (a feature which no later ship
was to have) and originally there were large Ladies' and Gentlemen's Cabins in the summer accommodation, but after the
Second War these were subdivided into two-berth cabins. The
St Magnus retained the straight stem which had become traditional, and bore the mark of her period in the shape of a
severe cruiser stern, so that on the whole she lacked the
beautiful profile of some earlier ships, but she was a handsome
vessel viewed from some angles. In 1956, when she was converted to oil-burning, a new, shorter funnel was fitted and it
did not improve her appearance. Apart from the single feature
of the cruiser stern, the *St Magnus* was an old-fashioned ship
even when she was built, for other lines were by that time
placing the first-class dining saloon under the bridge and the
second-class accommodation aft and not in the forecastle. But
if these were defects, they made her a remarkably spacious
ship, both on deck and below, for first-class passengers. Owing
to the arrangement whereby temporary berths could be made up
in the public rooms, this ship could provide beds for no less than
234 first-class passengers — a number considerably exceeding
the capacity of her larger successors.

    The *St Magnus* was the weekend boat in summer from
1924 to 1939, except in 1930, when, after the loss of the *St
Sunniva* (I), she was on the direct run. She was little used in
winter until 1937, when she appeared on the weekend run and
the direct run. In 1939-40 she was in the hands of the

Admiralty, and took part in the Norwegian campaign, but during most of the Second War, and until 1946, she ran mainly from Aberdeen to Lerwick, and was twice attacked by enemy aircraft — on 1 April 1941 off Tod Head and on 20 October 1942 five miles south-east of Fair Isle. On the former occasion the plane was so low that it carried away the ship's wireless aerial and damaged her masts, but no one was injured by its machine-gun fire and the gunners of the *St Magnus* put some shots into the plane, which was losing height as it made off. From 1946 the *St Magnus* took up what was now the principal indirect run, leaving Leith on Monday and returning on Saturday, until in 1950 she returned to her old weekend run, though it terminated at Kirkwall except in the summer months. In 1960 she was sold for breaking-up.

St Magnus (IV), *see* **St Clair** (II).

St Magnus (V) (970/1220). A cargo-only motor vessel, built in 1955 and sold in 1966 by Palgrave Murphy Ltd. to the North of Scotland Company, who changed her name from *City of Dublin* and made considerable alterations to provide refrigerated space and accommodation for livestock. She took up the service from Leith to Aberdeen and Kirkwall in March 1967 and after the withdrawal from Leith continued to trade mainly between Aberdeen and Kirkwall until 1977, when she was sold to Sunstar Lines, Cyprus, and renamed *Mitera*.

St Margaret (I) (943). Built by Ramage and Ferguson, she came into service in 1913 but operated on the direct run for only two summers before the outbreak of war and had the shortest career of any vessel built for the Company. While on charter to G. and J. Burns, Ltd., of Glasgow, she was torpedoed and sunk on 12 September 1917. The story of the survivors of the *St Margaret* was an example of fortitude and seamanship which attracted the attention of Joseph Conrad, who wrote an account of it in an article on 'Tradition' printed in his *Notes on Life and Letters*.[8] While on a voyage from Lerwick to Iceland, the ship was attacked without warning some thirty miles east of the Faroes. The torpedo exploded in the bunkers, and the ship went down in about four minutes. The chief officer, an A.B., a greaser and two firemen were drowned, the other eighteen members of the ship's company survived. Captain William

Leask, the last to leave the vessel, was sucked down as she sank and by an extraordinary stroke of ill-fortune he came to the surface underneath an overturned lifeboat, where a fireman was clinging already. They shouted to attract attention, and the members of the company who had gathered in another boat started to break through the hull of the overturned boat in an effort to liberate the two trapped men. The head of their axe flew off at the first stroke, and they had to use a boathook, so that it took half an hour to break through, and by that time the fireman had gone. The capain remained unconscious for several hours, but was brought back to consciousness and then found that an attempt had been made to row the boat, in the teeth of the wind, towards Faroe. He undertook to navigate over the much longer distance — over 150 miles — to Shetland, and the others agreed to make the attempt. With an oar for a mast and part of the boat's cover for a sail, they had a hazardous and miserable voyage before heavy seas and under a downpour of rain which compelled them for a time to take down the 'sail' and use it for shelter, but the navigation was precise, and they reached Hillswick in safety, after three days and nights in the boat. Captain Leask, who was also in command of the first *St Clair* when she had her encounter with a submarine a few months later, was decorated with the D.S.C.

St Margaret (II) (1105). Built in 1907, by the Ailsa Company, as the *Chieftain,* for David MacBrayne's cargo and cruising service from Glasgow to Stornoway, this vessel was described as 'a vision of beauty', with her yacht-like lines and clipper bow. Her passenger accommodation, with staterooms opening directly on to the deck, won high praise, but her career was not a success either with her original owners or with the North of Scotland Company, which bought her in 1919 and put her on the west-side service in summer from 1920 to 1924. Designed for the days of cheap coal, she was expensive to run after the First World War, and her lack of a well made her unhandy for the smaller ports where boats were employed, since all goods had to go in slings on the derricks. She was sold in 1925 to the Canadian National Steamship Company, of Prince Rupert, British Columbia, and renamed *Prince Charles*. In 1940 she passed to Union Steamships, Vancouver, as the *Camosun,* and before the end of the same year she was transferred again, to the Oriental Navigation Company of Tel Aviv, who named her *Cairo*. In 1947 she was sold to the Zarati Steamship Company and registered at Panama to trade between Marseilles and Beira. She was broken up at Spezia in 1952.[9]

St Nicholas (787).[10] An iron screw steamer, built at White-inch in 1871, she closely resembled the *St Clair* (I), and photographs of the two have sometimes been confused, but the two ships did in fact differ in the design of both bows and stern. It is obvious from their records as well as from their appearance that the two ships were peculiarly interchangeable, and between them they carried almost complete responsibility for the Caithness and west-side services for a great many years. The *St Nicholas* was on the Caithness run in summer and winter from 1871 to 1874, during the whole or part of the summer from 1876 to 1887 and in 1913, and in winter from 1877 to 1900. She was on the west side during part of the summer in most years from 1884 to 1905 and during all or part of the winter from 1896 to 1906, in 1911-12 and 1913-14; and in winter from 1907 to 1911 she was on the Stromness and Lerwick run. She appeared less regularly on the east side of the islands, but she ran to Kirkwall and Lerwick in summer intermittently from 1870 to 1899 and regularly from 1906 to 1912, and in winter she sometimes did the weekend run, relieving in 1885-7 and 1893-6. She pioneered the direct Aberdeen-Lerwick service in the summer of 1891. She ran aground at the entrance to Wick on 17 June 1914 and settled on a ledge, with the consequence that when the tide ebbed she became a total loss.[11]

St Ninian (I) (702). Built for the North of Scotland Company in 1895, she was at first the weekend boat, in summer 1895-6 and in winter 1895-1914, but from 1897 to 1905 she was the secondary indirect boat for the whole or part of each season, and it was to this route that she returned in the summers from 1920 to 1936. In her last three peacetime summers she succeeded the *St Clair* (I) on the Caithness runs. She served on the west side during part of the summer season in 1899 and the whole of it from 1906 to 1914 and in winter in 1902-3, and between the Wars she usually appeared there as a relief in spring or early summer. Between the Wars she was little used in winter. The only significant change in her appearance throughout her career was the erection of a small deck on top of the after deckhouse. Her war service was notable: during both the First World War and the Second World War she acted as a transport for naval personnel between Scrabster and Longhope; in the Second World War she crossed the Firth 3,000 times, steaming over 100,000 miles and carrying 900,000 persons. It was said that her engines never recovered from the hard usage they received in the First World War, and after it she was certainly a slow ship, even by the standards of that time. Although she was reliable and almost accident-free, she was never a popular ship. Her measurements (205 ft. by 28.6) do not suggest that she was unduly narrow — she was beamier than the first *St Clair* and the first *St Sunniva* — but there was some peculiarity in the design of her hull which, while it made her a good boat with a head sea, made her roll miraculously under other conditions. After the Second World War she was not brought back into regular service, but lay idle at Aberdeen for a long time until being broken up at Rosyth in 1948.

St Ninian (II) (2,242). The first major post-war vessel, built at Dundee in 1950, she was a twin-screw motor ship far exceeding in tonnage anything the Company had owned previously. She was at once appointed to the principal indirect run, leaving Leith on Monday and returning on Saturday, and served there throughout, except when she acted as a relief to the *St Clair* (II) on the direct Aberdeen-Lerwick run from 1951 to 1960 and 1968 to 1971. She was sold in 1971 to Atlantique Cruise Lines and refitted in Nova Scotia to begin cruises in June 1971 from North Sydney to St Pierre and Miquelon. The Atlantique Company went bankrupt in 1972 and the ship was tied up for four years, but in 1976 she was purchased by Galapagos Tourist Corporation, Ecuador, for cruises to the Galapagos Islands under the name *Buccaneer* — a curious fate for a 'Saint'.

St Ola (I) (231). A steel screw steamer, built by Hall, Russell and Co. of Aberdeen in 1892 for the Pentland Firth service, on which she remained throughout her long career. She grounded on Hunda on 4 July 1936 and was replaced for a week by the *St Clair* (I). She was broken up at Charlestown in 1951.

St Ola (II) (750). A motor ship, built by Hall, Russell and Co. in 1951 to succeed her namesake on the Pentland Firth. She relieved in the North Isles of Shetland. Early in 1975 she was sold to Aquatronics International Ltd. of Bermuda, who renamed her *Aqua Star* and converted her for North Sea oil operations.

St Ola (III) (1345). Built by Hall, Russell to succeed the second *St Ola* in 1975, she was the Company's first drive-through vehicle carrier. See chapter 5.

St Olaf (232). An iron screw steamer (130.9 ft. by 22.3), built at Port Glasgow in 1882 for the Pentland Firth service. She was sold in 1890 to G. R. Renfrew, Quebec, and lengthened by 20 feet, increasing her tonnage to 305. Sold again to A. Fraser, Quebec, in 1893, she was lost in 1900.

St Rognvald (I) (1053). An iron screw steamer, built in 1883, she operated the weekend run as her normal route throughout her career, in both summer and winter, but from 1886 onwards she was employed in a certain amount of seasonal cruising. Originally she had a well fore and aft, with the 'tween-decks designed as cargo space, and it was in this state (and still with a black funnel) that she first went to Norway. After cruising proved an immediate success, she underwent modification in two phases. The first step was to substitute a trunk for the after well and give her a flush deck from the stern to the bridge, with 22 two-berth rooms on the main deck amidships. Later, between 1894 and 1898, the deck house was extended further aft to create a 'music saloon' in addition to the smoking room, and this made possible the provision of a more extensive promenade deck on top, but no fresh changes were made in the layout of the main deck. At the first modification another two boats were added to the original four. The second illustration of the vessel in this book shows her after the first modification; the plan shows her after the second, and it was the foundation for the description in chapter 7. On 24 March 1891, while on passage from Lerwick to Kirkwall, the *St Rognvald* ran ashore in heavy snow on the Head of Work, near Kirkwall, but suffered little damage. On 24 April 1900, on passage from Lerwick to Kirkwall, she was wrecked in fog on Burgh Head, Stronsay.

St Rognvald (II) (923/1069). Built in 1901, she was an excellently designed ship for both passenger and cargo requirements and earned great popularity as a comfortable and reliable vessel. She succeeded her namesake on the weekend run in summer 1901-14 and during parts of some winters in that period; she was on this route again in summer 1919-24 and in 1930, and in winter 1919-36; and she returned to it, in truncated form, between 1946 and 1950. In the summers from 1925 to 1936 (except 1930) she was on the west side, and in the summer of 1950 she ran from Leith to Aberdeen and Stromness. From 1946 to 1950 she relieved the *St Magnus* on the Kirkwall and Lerwick run. She underwent hardly any change in her long career, but a deck shelter for passengers at the after end of the boat deck was not an original feature, and after the Second War it was converted into a wireless cabin. In her first season (10 September 1901) the *St Rognvald* struck Fair Isle and damaged her bows; and on 19 May 1934, while disembarking three passengers into a small boat on the west side of Fair Isle, she struck 'a submerged object' (later identified as Fugli Baa), but was able to proceed to Lerwick, where repairs were made to one or two plates and rivets. Indeed the *St Rognvald's* whole career was free from serious mishaps, and her luck held one day in the mid-1930s when she caused some excitement. She arrived off Aberdeen to find that port closed, but she had insufficient bunkers either to take her on to Leith or to run round into the Moray Firth for shelter; her master had no alternative but to take the risk of entering Aberdeen, and he succeeded in doing so. During the second War and until the summer of 1946 the *St Rognvald* maintained a service between Aberdeen and Orkney. On 27 December 1940 she was attacked by a captured British bomber with a German crew and on 30 April 1941 she was damaged in an air attack 22 miles north of Kinnaird Head, without casualties. She was broken up at Ghent in 1951.

St Rognvald (III) (1024). When this motor vessel was laid down she was intended to have accommodation for 50 passengers, but technical difficulties intervened and when she appeared in

1955 she had taken shape as a cargo vessel carrying only twelve passengers. She differed from her predecessors of that type by having the bridge and all accommodation aft. She was designed as the Company's principal livestock-carrier. During most of the year, except when being overhauled or making special trips to carry stock, she ran from Leith to Kirkwall (and Stromness until the service to the latter port was withdrawn), and during part of the winter she took over the weekend run from Leith to Aberdeen and Kirkwall. From 1967 her regular run came to be from Leith to Aberdeen and Kirkwall and from 1971 (when the regular service from Leith ended) her usual employment was Aberdeen-Kirkwall-Lerwick.

St Sunniva (I) (864). Some account of this vessel in her original form, as she was built by Hall, Russell and Co. for cruising in 1887, was given in chapter seven. Her dimensions were 236 ft. by 29.6 ft. The following description was provided for intending passengers in 1907:

> The whole space of the vessel is devoted to accommodation for first-class passengers. The engines are triple expansion, developing 2000 h.p. and giving a speed of fifteen knots. In the construction of all parts of the vessel, strength, combined with gracefulness of outline, have been considered, so as to give the necessary stability with a yacht-like appearance.
>
> The vessel is lighted throughout by electricity and furnished with electric bells. There is also a steam launch to facilitate the transport of passengers to and from the landing-places.
>
> The sleeping cabins are arranged, in most part, for two persons, but when required the upper bed may be removed, and the cabin made suitable for one.
>
> Every care has been taken to ensure perfect ventilation in all the cabins, while the internal arrangements are designed to supply all the required conveniences of their occupants.
>
> Most of the beds are fitted with patent spring mattresses, and, as will be seen from the accompanying plan of the vessel, there is large provision made in the shape of bath and lavatory accommodation.
>
> It should also be specially noticed that the captain,

officers and crew are all British seamen, who have been long in the Company's service, in which only thoroughly efficient and reliable men are employed.

The stewards, stewardess and cooks have been carefully chosen to promote in their several capacities the comfort of all on board.

When the ship was withdrawn from cruising, in 1908, she required considerable alteration to suit her for the regular passenger, mail and cargo service between Leith, Aberdeen and Lerwick. Two hatches were inserted, and all passenger accommodation removed from the lower deck. On the main deck, the dining saloon was reduced in size so that a ladies' cabin and other passenger accommodation could be provided, and the forward end of the accommodation space on the main deck was turned over to second-class passengers. On the upper deck, a number of four-berth staterooms were constructed amidships. Additional deck space for first-class passengers was provided on top of the after deckhouse, and a fifth boat (in addition to four carried on the boat deck) was placed on the port side of the after hatch. So altered, the ship ran on the direct route in summer and winter from 1909 to 1914 and again from 1919 to 1930. In October 1914 she was put on a run *via* Kirkwall. Although, after the First World War, her engines were never used to capacity, she had the reserve of speed which made her a good time-keeper on her exacting summer schedule — twice from Aberdeen to Lerwick and once from Aberdeen to Leith each week. She stranded near Graemeshall in Orkney in February 1914 and near Peterhead in 1928. She ran aground on Mousa in fog when on her way north from Aberdeen on the morning of 10 April 1930, and after about a fortnight she broke up.

St Sunniva (II) (1368). Launched from the yard of Hall, Russell and Company on 2 April 1931, almost exactly a year after the loss of her namesake, the second *St Sunniva* was larger than the first, with dimensions 267.5 ft. by 37 ft., but in her internal arrangements followed almost slavishly those of the first, and her hull carried out the clipper design to the full. While thus in a sense old-fashioned — it was unkindly said that she was obsolete from the day she was launched — the triumph of sentiment and beauty over utility had a certain appeal, and

31. *St Ninian (II)*

32　St. Clair (III)

33. *St Magnus (V)*

34. *Flit-boat, Burravoe*

the Company's decision to build such a ship, in the depths of industrial depression, captured the imagination. It was significant of the whole concept lying behind her design that on her maiden trip north she stopped off Mousa while all on board stood bareheaded to commemorate her predecessor. Her clipper bow carried a figurehead of the saint whose name she bore, with an outstretched arm which could be removed at sea to save it from damage. The ship was well fitted, handsome inside as well as out, and comfortable in her appointments, but was very lively in heavy seas. Her power was adequate for the rather slow timetable then prevailing, and she could do the trip from Lerwick to Leith, with a call at Aberdeen, in under twenty-four hours. She served on the direct run in summer from 1931 to 1937 and from that year until 1939 during part of the winter as well. In July 1937 she made an isolated run south *via* Kirkwall. She had a curious mishap at the end of August 1934. Making her usual weekly run, on Sunday, from Aberdeen to Leith, the chief officer omitted to alter course at the May Island. It was a fine evening, and some passengers were aware that the ship was on an unusual course, but she drove on. When Captain William Gifford came on the bridge, knowing that the ship was due to be approaching Leith, he found her heading for the island of Fidra, and was just in time to ring for reduced speed. She grounded, but no damage of any consequence was done. Commandeered before the outbreak of war (29 August 1939), the *St Sunniva*, after surviving various assignments and taking part in the Norwegian campaign, was lost on 21-2 January 1943, while serving as a rescue ship with a transatlantic convoy. She disappeared without trace, and the presumption was that her masts and rigging became encrusted with ice and she turned turtle. There were no survivors.

Sovereign (378/417). A wooden paddler, 158.7 ft. by 24.7 ft., built in 1836, she inaugurated the steamer service to Lerwick in the summer of that year and continued on the run from Leith to Aberdeen, Wick, Kirkwall and Lerwick each summer for ten years. In the summer of 1849 she ran from Leith to Aberdeen and in summer 1850-61 from Leith to Wick or (in 1851 and 1859) to Inverness. In winter she was little used until 1848, when she was put on the Leith-Aberdeen service; in 1849 she ran to Inverness in winter, and most winters 1850-61 she ran

I

to Wick; but when the winter service to Lerwick started, in 1858, she appeared from time to time on that run, until 1861. In 1865 she was sold to J. B. Adam, Aberdeen, and later in the same year to F. T. Barry, London, and others. She was stranded on Arklow Bank on 12 January 1872, and after being refloated was sold to E. Kearon, Arklow, who removed her engines. On 7 January 1901, while being operated by Cardiff owners, she was wrecked at Muros, Spain.

Temaire (438). Built for the Garnock S.S. Company, Ayr, as *Burnock,* in 1890, she was sold in 1899 to A. Weir and Company, Glasgow, and to James McKelvie, Glasgow, in 1915, when she was renamed. With the North of Scotland Company in 1916 and 1917, she subsequently passed through various hands, as *Innisholm* and *Austin Gough,* before being broken up in 1931.

Vanguard (608). An iron paddler, built in 1843 for the Dublin and Glasgow sailings of the Steam Packet Company of Dublin, she was acquired by the Aberdeen, Leith and Clyde in May 1863, and ran mainly to Caithness, in summer and winter, 1864-7, but to Lerwick in the summer of 1863 and part of the summer of 1867. She was broken up in 1868.

Velocity (149). A wooden paddler, built at Dumbarton in in 1821 for service between Aberdeen and Leith, where she operated 1821-32 and 1836-8. She inaugurated the service from Leith and Aberdeen to Wick and Kirkwall in 1833 and continued on it in summer until 1835. In that year she was refitted by I. and W. Napier, Glasgow, and in the summer of 1838 sailed from Leith to Aberdeen and Inverness. She was sold in 1844 to the Aberdeen and Newcastle Steam Navigation Company. She stranded on Aberdeen pier on 25 October 1848 and became a total loss.

Victory (92). A wooden paddler, built in 1844 and acquired by the Aberdeen, Leith and Clyde in 1847. She was sold to Liverpool owners in 1860.

REFERENCES

1   There was an earlier vessel of this name, Stromness owned, in 1851, and an *Earl of Zetland* arrived at Kirkwall from Liverpool on 10 May 1860. See also p. 8.

2   See Chapter 5. There is a full biography of this ship in Cormacks, *Days of Orkney Steam,* 221-2, and an illustration in *Marine News,* xix, 316.

3   The *Cavalier* is illustrated in Duckworth and Langmuir, *West Highland Steamers.*

4   There is a model of the *Prince Consort* in the Lerwick Museum. The illustration which appeared as Plate 1 in the first edition of this book, with a possible identification as the *Prince Consort,* seems in fact not to be of that vessel.

4a A photograph of the *St Clair* (I) in her later days was reproduced in the first edition of this book.

5   There was at least one sailing vessel of this name. A *St Clement* appears in the Aberdeen Harbour Records in 1838; and in 1885 a *St Clement,* of 39 registered tons, was owned by Thomas Walker, Aberdeen.

6   There was an earlier *St Fergus,* owned at Wick in 1857.

7   There was a Kirkwall-owned sailing ship of this name in 1861. The successive steamships of the name are the subject of an article by Alastair McRobb in *Ships Illustrated* in June and July 1965; they give full details and have many fine illustrations, including one of the interior of the saloon of the first *St Magnus.*

8   My attention was drawn to this by Captain Leask's son, Mr R. M. Leask, who also lent me several papers relating to his father's career, including the Captain's own account of the loss of the *St Margaret.* A narrative was printed in the *Mercantile Marine Service Association Reporter* for June 1918.

9   There is a fine picture of the *Chieftain* in Duckworth and Langmuir, *West Highland Steamers.* During her North of Scotland service her funnel was for a time black and for a time yellow, as photographs show.

10 There was a wooden barque of this name, of 140 tons, built in 1834 for I. Abernethy and Co. of Aberdeen and acquired in 1844 by Richard Cannon and Co., also of Aberdeen. She ran to London in the 1850s.

11 A painting of the *St Nicholas* was reproduced in the first edition of this book.

PART III

EPILOGUE

EPILOGUE

The history of powered navigation up and down the east coast of Scotland and to and from the northern islands now extends over more than a century and a half, and must be seen in the context of the whole developments in transport during that period. For a brief space, steam navigation had hardly any competitor at all, for it offered every advantage over the only alternative, namely horse-drawn transport. When the railways came, they made a difference, but their effect was less immediate, and more limited, than is apt to be thought. It is true that the opening of the railway between Aberdeen and Inverness in 1858 was almost immediately followed by the withdrawal of the steamer service between those ports (though the direct railway line from Perth to Inverness was not opened until 1863). On the other hand, while the opening of the railway to Aberdeen in 1850 must have reduced the utility of the steamer service from Leith, the steamers long remained serious rivals to the trains. The train journey from Edinburgh to Aberdeen was relatively slow until the Tay and Forth Bridges were built towards the end of the century and even thereafter the length of the sea voyage — 6 hours or even less in the days of hard steaming — did not greatly exceed the 4 hours or so which the train usually took until a few years ago. The steamer fare was cheaper than the train, the reduced fares offered at holiday seasons were particularly attractive, many people thought a trip to Aberdeen by sea in day-time was not a bad way to begin or end a holiday, and right to the end there were discerning business men who appreciated the convenience of an overnight voyage from Leith to Aberdeen. It was also noticeable that the steamers for a long time maintained their rivalry with the slow and tortuous train journey from Edinburgh or from Aberdeen to Wick and Thurso, although they were reached by the railway in 1874.

The coming of the internal combustion engine, however,

radically altered the situation. The drastic undercutting by the buses of the passenger fares on trains and steamers alike, and the convenience offered by a 'door to door' service for goods by motor lorry, brought road transport to the front. The fares by sea between Leith and Aberdeen were appreciably lower than the railway fares as long as the service operated, but they could not compete with the bus fares, and the buses attracted the type of traveller who used to go by sea — the man who hoped to save some money at the cost of spending a longer time on the journey. And, of course, goods traffic between ports on the Scottish mainland virtually came to an end.

The internal combustion engine led to the aeroplane as well as the bus and lorry. From its introduction, air travel to and from the islands attracted those who were fearful of a sea voyage, and it has continued to appeal to those who believe — sometimes mistakenly — that it will get them to their destination more quickly than the boat. The fact that the planes offer a daily service has, of course, been a strong point in their favour. Passenger traffic by sea in winter between Aberdeen and Orkney was almost eliminated by the air service, and even to Shetland it was greatly reduced. Yet the total number of trips made by ordinary passengers rose from 47,396 in 1938 to 59,533 in 1961. After that it fell to 55,961 in 1965. That the ships continued to be full to capacity in summer was due mainly to the expansion of the tourist business: trips made by cruise passengers numbered only 3510 in 1939 and 3537 ten years later, whereas the figure for 1961 was 16,053 and for 1965 it was 19,894. With the withdrawal of several passenger ships in succeeding years the numbers fell away, but the drive-through facilities for cars have brought the passengers back: the number of passenger journeys from January to September 1977 was 31,988, an increase of 36% over 1976.

Until 1939 there were numerous regular passenger and cargo services on the east coast — from London to Leith (two companies, running altogether six ships each week each way), to Grangemouth, to Dundee and to Aberdeen, and from Hull and Newcastle to Aberdeen. Of all those fleets, the ships of the North of Scotland Company were the last survivors. Also until 1939 there were passenger vessels on other parts of the British coast, offering the equivalent of cruises from London to Glasgow, London to Liverpool, Glasgow to the Western Isles and so on. The last survivors were two Coast Line vessels which conveyed twelve passengers in the summer months between London and Liverpool, and after they ceased to operate about 1967 the North of Scotland ships became the only vessels offering cruises of any duration on the coasts of Britain. Official policy, for whatever reason, is aimed at fostering road and air transport at the expense of sea and rail transport, and the present generation must be the first since the history of civilised man began that has neglected that natural highway which, at no cost whatever in construction and maintenance, could convey goods and passengers safely between one port and another.

Viewed against this background, the record of the Company which has so long served the north of Scotland and the northern isles is the more remarkable. Until only a few years ago, when it became necessary to seek government assistance for the maintenance of the service to the North Isles of Shetland, the Company had always operated successfully without any government aid whatever — except, of course, the modest payment allowed for the conveyance of the mails. In this respect, its record has been conspicuously different from that of the services to the western isles of Scotland. The latter have been heavily subsidised for a long time, and it became apparent as early as 1928 that a service to that area on a commercial profit-making basis was out of the question.

This great achievement of private enterprise in an age of nationalisation and subsidies is the more admirable when account is taken of the cost of replacing tonnage, which has become the critical factor. This problem quite defeated MacBrayne's, whose car-ferries, when they appeared, were built by the government and leased to the Company, and the same was true of Orkney Steam, as explained in chapter 5. The North of Scotland, by contrast, was able to shoulder an ambitious building programme after World War II, at a time when costs had risen spectacularly. The first St Ola had cost only about £10,000; the second St Ola — admittedly a much superior vessel, but still a replacement along the lines which the standards of the time demanded — cost about £150,000. The St Magnus (III) had cost about £80,000, and her value when sold for scrap was only £20,000; but she was replaced by the St Clair (III), which cost nearly a million, and it was remarked that her stabilisers cost nearly as much as the entire *St Magnus* had done. Operating costs have risen correspondingly: we have come a long way from the days when (even in the 1930s) Davie Gray calculated that he could take the old *Earl* from Lerwick to Aberdeen for £50.

Not the least of the virtues of sea travel is its safety. It appears from the available evidence that never in the history of the 'North Company' and its predecessors and successors in powered navigation has any passenger lost his life through a mishap to a ship in peacetime, and very few indeed of the ships' officers and crews have ever been casualties. Even in the course of the two World Wars, the losses were very small. If people were not so utterly indifferent to the appalling toll of the roads, they might better appreciate safety as a recommendation of sea transport.

It is not to be denied that passengers have sometimes had hair-raising experiences, and among many 'bad nights' and 'bad days' (so called with the Shetlander's gift for understatement) a few are particularly memorable, even within the last fifty years or so. In October 1926 the *St Rognvald* (II) was 33 hours on the passage from Aberdeen to Kirkwall — three times the normal. That was not, indeed, a record for that ship, because at the beginning of August 1931 she was 72 hours from Aberdeen to Stromness, but this was because of fog and she spent most of the time lying in Sinclair's Bay. In the autumn of 1927 the *St Ninian* (I), when off Duncansby Head on her way from Aberdeen to Stromness, was swept by a huge tidal lump which flooded the ladies' cabin and put out the fire in the galley. The *St Sunniva* (I) had a bad time in her last winter (1929-30): leaving Lerwick for Aberdeen she encountered weather which did damage on deck and the captain performed the difficult task of turning her in the heavy sea and putting back to Lerwick; she lay in Lerwick harbour for five days — much to the detriment of fowls and other fresh meat which were in the Christmas mail destined by Shetlanders for their friends in the south. Reference was made in chapter 4 to the experience of the *St Catherine* in the great storm of January 1937. One of the passengers was the late Sheriff Wallace, who wrote me after the appearance of the first edition of this book giving an account of many of his voyages in fog and storm, in peace and war. He wrote as follows: 'I was three times hove to at sea, in *St Rognvald* when a port hole was smashed in, in *St Clair* when in a bad storm one January cattle had to be sorted out off Fair Isle and I had the curious experience of going on hands and knees to fix a slamming cupboard door and was just reaching it when I and the carpet beneath me slid backwards underneath the bunk. The worst do was on the *Catherine* in 1937, when we set off from Aberdeen with the storm cone up. I was in a deck cabin and after seeing water coming in over the top of the door and picking my shoes up as they floated past, Hamish Tait (the purser) and some stewards arrived and said I must go below as if another like that came aboard the cabin might go over the side. So I and a Department of Health doctor were housed in the Ladies' Cabin. In the morning the Doctor said I was younger than him, "Look out of the port and see if you can see Lerwick". I got out and was flung against the side, and holding on to the port I said I could see nothing but the most horrible mountains of dark grey water, and what was more, we were not going. So that meant 13 hours hove to, steaming 3 knots and being driven westwards. To shorten a fearsome tale, about 5 p.m., poised on a mountain of water, I saw a flash of a lighthouse, also spotted by Captain Gifford on the bridge. It was Fair Isle and he decided to have a go for Lerwick and we dropped anchor about 9 that night and had a good supper as I was very hungry. A couple were anxious to get ashore as their son was gravely ill in hospital, so we Aldis-lamped the harbour. There was a trawler and some Lerwick men made up for missing crew ashore, and she made about 8 knots to get alongside, and finally hit the ancient Catherine such a bang that I thought she would stove in her side. Then we had to jump from the rail to the trawler, being cushioned on landing by the nets and caught by the crew. On shore a taxi man said, "You will be wanting to go out to Westhall, Sheriff". When I said "Yes", he said "The sea road has been washed away in nine places". And it was so. In places it was just a concrete parapet with nothing underneath'. I recall that a newspaper report on that grim morning on the *St Catherine,* of which the Sheriff wrote so vividly, noted with restraint that 'Breakfast, served in the saloon, was not a success'.

Despite the conditions which such accounts reveal, there has been no case of a ship foundering at sea. Most of the strandings and losses of ships have occurred through fog, and no doubt each of them was the result of an error of judgment, but it says much for the skill of the masters that the mishaps have been so few. The standard of accuracy in navigation, generation after generation, is beyond all praise.

One can only speculate about how much lore, how many lessons of experience, were passed on from one generation of officers to another. The routes through the islands included some narrow and tortuous channels which could be safely navigated only by the use of leading marks or 'meads' as Shetlanders call them, and which therefore could not be used in darkness or fog. On heading north out of Kirkwall, for instance, it was possible to pass between Shapinsay and the Skerry of Vasa by keeping the Cathedral Tower astern over the east end of Shapinsay. Some such 'meads' were certainly handed on from skipper to skipper, others were worked out by individual masters from their own observations and calculations. Besides, meads were often used in clear weather simply as a matter of convenience, in preference to compass bearings. Anyone can see from the chart that on coming out of Uyea-sound a bearing of the Hill of Clibberswick over Balta Light carried the ship safely outside the Colvidale Baas and the Vere. But it took more than a glance at a chart to determine some of the more picturesque meads. It was illuminating to stand in the wheelhouse of the *Earl* and hear orders like 'The Skerry' and 'The Tyres' when approaching Symbister from the north (the Tyres being the enormous tyres hung from the west end of the pier as fenders); but the uninitiated found it cryptic to hear the order 'Peter Ned's hut' when approaching Baltasound. 'The kirk ower the kailyard' was a bearing on the route through Whalsay Sound, and on the tortuous approach to Lerwick from the north the Town Hall was the mark twice over. Every rock had its bearings: the position of the Unicorn Rock, on which Kirkcaldy of Grange lost his ship in 1567, was defined by Score Head over Green Holm and the Ward of Clett over the Mull of Eswick; that much, again, anyone can see from the chart, but the point is that the *Earl's* skipper carried a multitude of such bearings in his head, giving him something like a mental map of the sea-bed. In thick weather, before the days of radar, the skipper had to rely much on his watch and count the minutes before changing course — it might be three minutes in fair conditions, five with a stiff head wind — but at least at one point, in the twisty north entrance to Lerwick, one course had a duration of 29 revolutions of the old *Earl's* propeller. Another device to which recourse was had before the days of radar was to sound the whistle and judge the distance from the cliffs by the time it took to hear the echo.

No doubt there were always captains and captains, those who had and those who lacked the special flair, the touch of instinct or genius, which went beyond any mere calculation. I recall, one Friday night in 1935, an experience on the *St Magnus* (III). She ran into fog as we neared Orkney, but Captain William Leask held on, with every mark of caution but with a perfectly sure touch. As we neared Kirkwall, the tall shape of the *St Ninian* (I) emerged from the gloom. I thought at first she was on her way out of Kirkwall, which she had been due to leave at 5 p.m., but as we came up to her I saw that she was at anchor; even so, I thought that she had been into Kirkwall. The *St Magnus* went on to Kirkwall pier, worked her cargo there and got safely away, still in fog, to find the *St Ninian* still lying at anchor — and she had never even been into Kirkwall.

Navigational aids have multiplied since that trip, when Captain Leask had a man in the chains constantly taking soundings. The *St Clair* (II) was the first ship to have an echo-meter, and since World War II all the ships have had radar. With radar, the situation has been transformed, though radar is merely an aid to navigation, not a substitute for it, and radar does not, in all conditions, make things as simple as the non-expert is apt to think. But even if fog has lost many of its dangers, the command of any of the North of Scotland ships still gives plenty of opportunity for skill of the highest order. For example, one never ceased to marvel at the precise judgment which could take one of the large modern ships through the narrow passage between Lerwick breakwater and Victoria Pier when a strong tide was running and the wind blowing up or down the harbour, a task which not infrequently gave trouble even in the days when ships had little more than half the beam of the *St Clair* (III). Equally, something to be wondered at is the coolness which can keep a ship in control when dashing into Aberdeen before a heavy following sea. The officers very properly get the credit, for they have the responsibility. But it would be less than fair to ignore the support they have from experienced crews, illustrated in an oft-told story (for the truth of which I cannot vouch): when the officer gave the order 'Starboard', the bo'sun at the wheel protested, 'Na, Sir, no yit'.

ADDITIONAL NOTE

At the end of 1977 P. & O. Ferries acquired the *Dorset* (1120 tons), a vehicle carrier with accommodation for twelve passengers, to operate mainly from Aberdeen to Stromness and Lerwick. She relieved the *St Clair* (IV) on the direct run in February-March 1978. This vessel was re-named *St Magnus,* and so became the sixth ship to bear that designation. Her arrival, and the prospective disposal of the *St Rognvald* (III), will apparently mean the end of a regular service to Kirkwall.

Perhaps a little ironically, this news almost coincided with a striking illustration of the continuing value of the flexibility of sea transport. In January 1978, when Caithness was completely cut off from the south because both roads and railways were blocked by snow, the *St Ola* (III) was able to make a trip to Aberdeen and so short-circuit the obstacles on land.

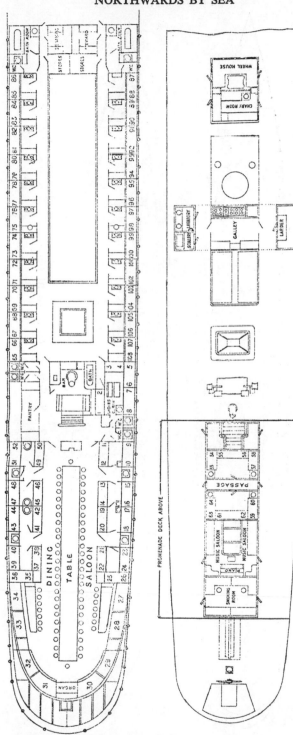

Plan 1. *St Rognvald (I)*

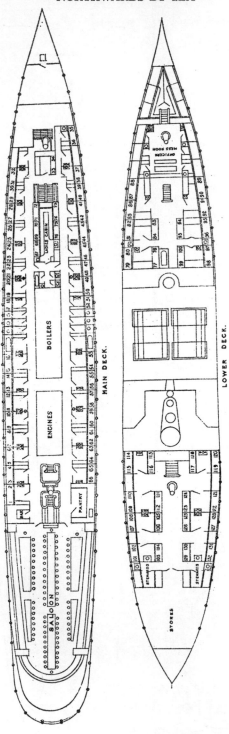

Plan 2.   *St Sunniva (I)* as yacht

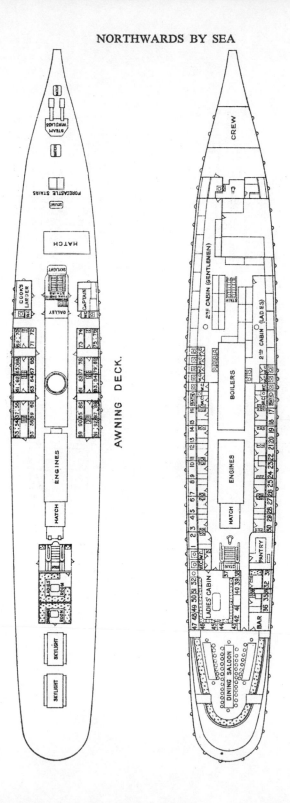

Plan 3. *St Sunniva (I)* as mail steamer

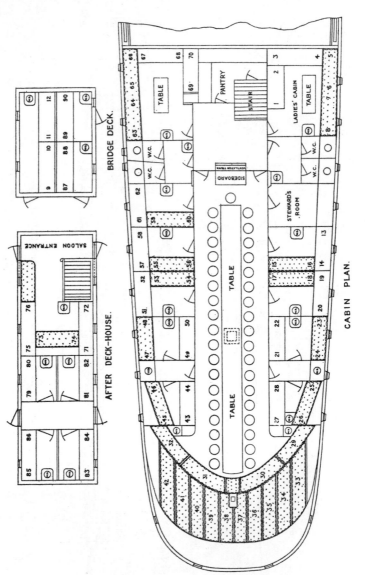

Plan 4. *St Catherine (I)*

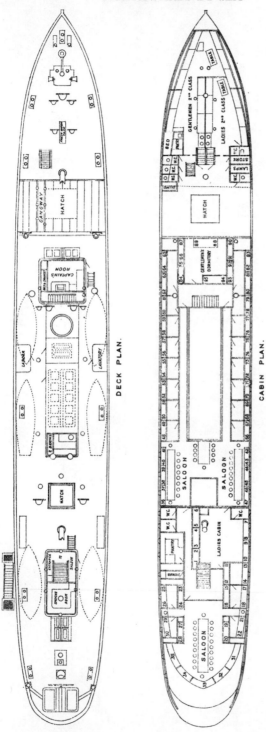

DECK PLAN.

CABIN PLAN.

Plan 5. *St Ninian (I)*

(The layout of the *St Rognvald* (II) was almost identical, but she had four staterooms in the after deckhouse and a Gents' Cabin and a Ladies' Cabin in place of the "Gentlemen's Dormitory".)

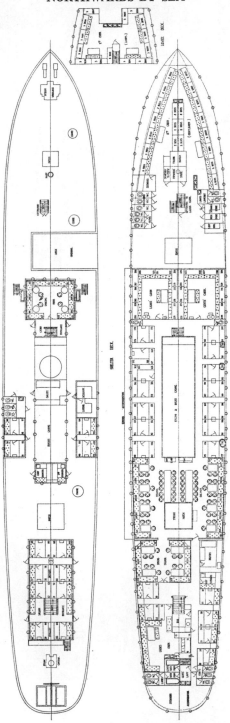

Plan 6. *St Magnus (III)*

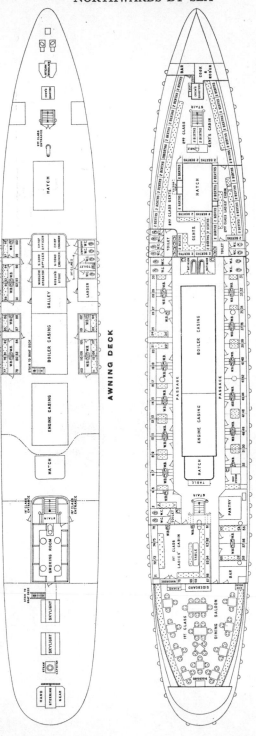

Plan 7. *St Sunniva (II)*

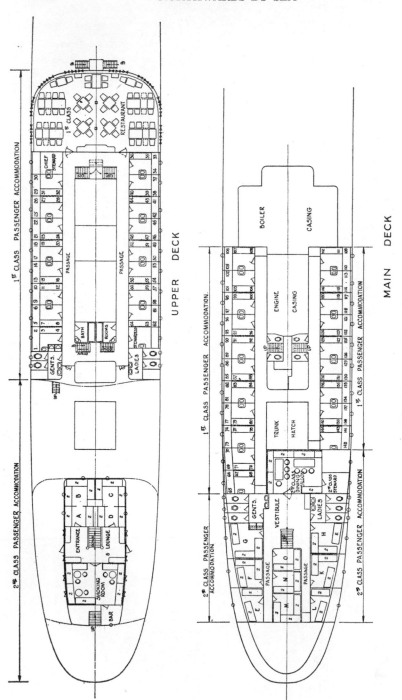

Plan 8. *St Clair (II)*

Note: On the promenade deck there was a 'covered promenade' surrounding a 1st Class lounge, above the 1st Class restaurant, and a 1st Class smoking room further aft.